LIFE BEFORE **LIFE**

LIFE BEFORE **LIFE**

Children's Memories of Previous Lives

Jim. B. Tucker, M.D.

With a Foreword by

Ian Stevenson, M.D.

ST. MARTIN'S GRIFFIN

NEW YORK

 Printed in the United States of America. For information, address St. Martin's Press, 175 Fifth Avenue, New York, N.Y. 10010.

www.stmartins.com

Library of Congress Cataloging-in-Publication Data

Tucker, Jim B.

Life before life : children's memories of previous lives / Jim B. Tucker.

p. cm.

Includes bibliographical references (p. 245).

ISBN-13: 978-0-312-37674-1

ISBN-10: 0-312-37674-X

1. Stevenson, Ian. 2. Reincarnation—Case studies. 3. Memory in children—Miscellanea—Case studies. I. Title.

BL515 T77 2005

133.9'01'35—dc22

2005047704

First published as *Life Before Life: A Scientific Investigation of Children's Memories of Previous Lives*

10 9 8 7 6 5 4 3

For Chris

CONTENTS

FOREWORD BY IAN STEVENSON, M.D.

Numerous authors have written about reincarnation, nearly always affirming it, some of them even purporting to describe its processes; a few writers dismiss the idea of reincarnation as absurd. Few of these authors seem interested in the question of evidence for or against reincarnation.

Jim Tucker has written a different kind of book. For him evidence has become central. Does it, he asks, support or even compel a belief in reincarnation?

One can easily think of objections to reincarnation: the paucity of persons who actually claim to remember a past life, the fragility of memories, the population explosion, the mind-body problem, fraud, and others. Jim Tucker discusses these, one by one and thoroughly. His book resembles no other, because it has no predecessor of its type.

I found particularly impressive Jim Tucker's guidance of his readers. He asks, almost requires, them to reason along with him as he describes and discusses each objection to the idea of reincarnation. He writes so well that he may beguile a casual reader into thinking he or she has no work to do. Read on, and learn that evidence may answer—sooner than you expected—the most important question we can ask ourselves: "What happens after death?"

INTRODUCTION

Some young children say that they have been here before. They give various details about previous lives, often describing the way in which they died. Of course, young children say a lot of things, and we may simply think that they are fantasizing as children often do. But what if, in a number of instances, people listened to the children and then tried to find out if the events they described had actually happened? And what if, when those people went to the places the children had named, they found that what the children had said about the past events was indeed true? What then?

The Case of Kemal Atasoy

Dr. Jürgen Keil, a psychologist from Australia, listened as Kemal Atasoy, a six-year-old boy in Turkey, confidently recounted details of a previous life that he claimed to remember. They were meeting in the boy's home, a comfortable house in an upper middle class neighborhood, and with them were Dr. Keil's interpreter and Kemal's parents, a well-educated couple who seemed amused at times by the enthusiasm that the little boy showed in describing his experiences. He said that he had lived in Istanbul, 500 miles away. He stated that his family's name had been Karakas and that he had been a rich Armenian Christian who lived in a large three-story house. The house, he said, was next to the house of a woman named Aysegul, a well-known personality in Turkey, who had left the country because of legal problems. Kemal said that his house had been on the water, where boats were tied up, and that a church was behind it. He said that his wife and children had Greek first names. He also said that he often carried a large leather bag and that he only lived in the house for part of the year.

No one knew if Kemal's story was true when he met Dr. Keil in 1997. His parents did not know anyone in Istanbul. In fact, Kemal and his mother had never been there, and his father had only visited the city twice on business. In addition, the family knew no Armenians. His parents were Alevi Muslims, a group with a belief in reincarnation, but they did not seem to think that Kemal's statements, which he had been making from the time he was just a toddler at two years of age, were particularly important.

Dr. Keil set out to determine if the statements that Kemal had given fit with someone who had actually lived. The work that Dr. Keil had to perform to find out if such a person even existed demonstrates that Kemal could not have come across the details of the man's life by accident.

When Dr. Keil and his interpreter went to Istanbul, they found the house of Aysegul, the woman whom Kemal had named. Next to the house was an empty three-story residence that precisely matched Kemal's description—it was at the edge of the water, where boats were tied up, with a church behind it. Dr. Keil then had trouble finding any evidence that a person like the one Kemal described had ever lived there. No Armenians were living in that part of Istanbul at the time, and Dr. Keil could not find anyone who remembered any Armenians ever having lived there. When he returned to Istanbul later that year, he talked with Armenian church officials, who told him that they were not aware that an Armenian had ever lived in the house. No church records indicated one had, but a fire had destroyed many of the records. Dr. Keil talked with an elderly man in the neighborhood who said that an Armenian had definitely lived there many years before and that the church officials were simply too young to remember that long ago.

Armed with that report, Dr. Keil decided to continue his search for information. The next year, he made a third trip to the area and interviewed a well-respected local historian. During the interview, Dr. Keil made sure he did not prompt any answers or make any suggestions. The historian told a story strikingly similar to the one Kemal had told. The historian said that a rich Armenian Christian had, in fact, lived in that house. He had been the only Armenian in that area, and his family's name was Karakas. His wife was Greek Orthodox, and her family did not approve of the marriage. The couple had three children, but the historian did not know their names. He said that the Karakas clan lived in another part of Istanbul, that they dealt in leather goods, and that the deceased man in question often carried a large leather bag. He also said that the deceased man lived in the house only during the summer months of the year. He had died in 1940 or 1941.

Though Dr. Keil was not able to verify Kemal's statement that the wife and children had Greek first names, the wife came from a Greek family. The first name that Kemal had given for the man turned out to be an Armenian term meaning "nice man."

Dr. Keil could not confirm that people actually called Mr. Karakas that, but he was struck by the fact that, even though no one around him knew the expression, Kemal had given a name that could easily have been used to describe Mr. Karakas.

How did this little boy, living in a town 500 miles away, know so many things about a man who had died in Istanbul fifty years before he was born? He could not have heard about the man Dr. Keil had to work so hard to learn anything about. What possible explanation could there be? Kemal had a very simple answer: he said that he had been the man in a previous life.

Kemal is not alone in his claims. Children all over the world have described memories of previous lives. For more than forty years, researchers have investigated their reports. More than 2,500 cases are registered in the files of the Division of Personality Studies at the University of Virginia. Some of the children have said they were deceased family members, and others described previous lives as strangers. In a typical case, a very young child begins to describe memories of another life. The child is persistent about this and often demands to be taken to his other family in another location. When the child has given names or enough details about the other location, the family often goes there to find that the child's statements fit the life of a person who has died in the recent past.

Were Kemal and the other 2,500 children remembering what they thought they were remembering—events from lives they had previously experienced? That question has occupied researchers for years, and this book will attempt to answer it. Previously, we have only written for a scientific audience, but now that we have forty years' worth of data, the general public deserves the opportunity to evaluate the evidence as well. I will try to present it in as fair a way as possible so that you can judge for yourself. The phenomenon of young children reporting past-life memories is fascinating in and of itself, and as you learn about it, you can gradually form an opinion about what it means. You can eventually decide whether you think that children like Kemal really have come back after having previous lives—and whether the rest of us may be able to come back, too.

LIFE BEFORE **LIFE**

CHAPTER 1

Children Who Report Memories of Previous Lives

John McConnell, a retired New York City policeman working as a security guard, stopped at an electronics store after work one night in 1992. He saw two men robbing the store and pulled out his pistol. Another thief behind a counter began shooting at him. John tried to shoot back, and even after he fell, he got up and shot again. He was hit six times. One of the bullets entered his back and sliced through his left lung, his heart, and the main pulmonary artery, the blood vessel that takes blood from the right side of the heart to the lungs to receive oxygen. He was rushed to the hospital but did not survive.

John had been close to his family and had frequently told one of his daughters, Doreen, "No matter what, I'm always going to take care of you." Five years after John died, Doreen gave birth to a son named William. William began passing out soon after he was born. Doctors diagnosed him with a condition called pulmonary valve atresia, in which the valve of the pulmonary artery has not adequately formed, so blood cannot travel through it to the lungs. In addition, one of the chambers of his heart, the right ventricle, had not formed properly as a result of the problem with the valve. He underwent several surgeries. Although he will need to take medication indefinitely, he has done quite well.

William had birth defects that were very similar to the fatal wounds suffered by his grandfather. In addition, when he became old enough to talk, he began talking about his grandfather's life. One day when he was three years old, his mother was at home trying to work in her study when William kept acting up. Finally, she told him, "Sit down, or I'm going to spank you." William replied, "Mom, when you were a little girl and I was your daddy, you were bad a lot of times, and I never hit you!"

His mother was initially taken aback by this. As William talked more about the life of his grandfather, she began to feel comforted by the idea that her father had returned. William talked about being his grandfather a number of times and discussed his death. He told his mother that several people were shooting during the incident when he was killed, and he asked a lot of questions about it.

One time, he said to his mother, "When you were a little girl and I was your daddy, what was my cat's name?" She responded, "You mean Maniac?"

"No, not that one," William answered. "The white one."

"Boston?" his mom asked.

"Yeah," William responded. "I used to call him Boss, right?" That was correct. The family had two cats, named Maniac and Boston, and only John referred to the white one as Boss.

One day, Doreen asked William if he remembered anything about the time before he was born. He said that he died on Thursday and went to heaven. He said that he saw animals there and also talked to God. He said, "I told God I was ready to come back, and I got born on Tuesday." Doreen was amazed that William mentioned days since he did not even know his days of the week without prompting. She tested him by saying, "So, you were born on a Thursday and died on Tuesday?" He quickly responded, "No, I died Thursday at night and was born Tuesday in the morning." He was correct on both counts—John died on a Thursday, and William was born on a Tuesday five years later.

He talked about the period between lives at other times. He told his mother, "When you die, you don't go right to heaven. You go to different levels—here, then here, then here" as he moved his hand up each time. He said that animals are reborn as well as humans and that the animals he saw in heaven did not bite or scratch.

John had been a practicing Roman Catholic, but he believed in reincarnation and said that he would take care of animals in his next life. His grandson, William, says that he will be an animal doctor and will take care of large animals at a zoo.

William reminds Doreen of her father in several ways. He loves books, as his grandfather did. When they visit William's grandmother, he can spend hours looking at books in John's study, duplicating his grandfather's behavior from years before. William, like his grandfather, is good at putting things together and can be a "nonstop talker."

William especially reminds Doreen of her father when he tells her, "Don't worry, Mom. I'll take care of you."

The idea that research could actually support the concept of reincarnation is surprising to many people in the West, since reincarnation may seem foreign or even absurd. People sometimes joke about their past lives or about their next one. The media document people dramatically describing lives from ancient times after being hypnotized. Reincarnation conflicts with the view of the majority of scientists that the material world is all that exists, and with many people's religious beliefs.

Although some people find the idea of reincarnation to be ridiculous or offensive, others accept it on faith. The idea of reincarnation has appealed to many throughout history and into the present day, including Plato and the ancient Greeks, Hindus and Buddhists in Asia, various West Africans, many Native Americans in northwest North America, and even some groups of early Christians. Today, people in the world who believe in reincarnation may outnumber those who do not.

Such beliefs are not restricted to distant places. A surprising number of Americans believe in reincarnation—between 20 and 27 percent, depending on the poll—and a similar percentage of Europeans do as well. They cannot base this belief on the evidence for reincarnation since most people do not know about this research done at the University of Virginia. They often do not base it on formal religious doctrine since many believers attend churches that do not hold such a view. In fact, a Harris poll in 2003 found that 21 percent of Christians in the United States believe in reincarnation. The work described here may give such individuals support for their beliefs, but the researchers have not operated from the perspective of any particular religious doctrine or bias. Our goals have been to determine the best explanation for the statements by the children and to see if science should consider reincarnation as a possibility.

Most people probably hope that the answer is yes. After all, the idea that we cease to exist when we die is unsettling for many of us. Though many in the United States may not be comfortable with the concept of reincarnation, the idea that part of us continues after we die is certainly appealing. If a deceased individual can survive death in some form and be reborn, then this means that we can continue on. Perhaps we can stay close to loved ones as they continue their lives or perhaps go to heaven or to other dimensions or who knows what. If these children are correct when they report that they lived before, then a part of us can survive the death of our bodies.

More specifically, the concept of reincarnation is compelling because the idea of being able to come back to try again may appeal to a lot of people. We cannot change the mistakes we have made in the past, but being able to try to do better the next time would certainly be a comfort. If we get to live repeated lives, then perhaps we can make progress across lifetimes and become better people.

As much as we might wish to come back ourselves, we also wish that the people we love could do so. Surely, William's mother must have been thrilled and comforted by her impression that her adoring father survived death and was reborn as her son. She had to deal with the horror of knowing that her father was murdered, and the idea that he was reborn as her son undoubtedly helped her change her grief into acceptance. We will meet others in this book who have dealt with similar losses: for example, a mother who watched her toddler die from cancer and a man whose father was closed off from his children before he died. In such situations, people would love the possibility of a second chance, of another opportunity to love and to share moments with the person who died. When any of us grieve for loved ones we have lost, we would certainly be comforted to know that those people have continued in some form and that they may come back into our lives.

Believing in that possibility may seem like wishful thinking and nothing more. But could life after death be more than wishful thinking?

Even though it may seem hard to believe, evidence might exist that life after death is actually a reality. *Life Before Life* will describe the cases researchers have collected that suggest that some people can survive death and be reborn into another life. This is not work that we have undertaken lightly. Researchers have addressed this issue with the same open-minded analytical approach that we would use with any question. We have approached the work rationally instead of emotionally, so it is analytical rather than emotional. In addition, we have done this work with clearheaded care, not with religious zeal. Of course, many people believe in life after death based purely on their religious faith. Though I mean to take nothing away from faith, religious belief need not keep us from looking for evidence that supports the idea. Faith should not prevent us from trying to gain a better understanding of the nature of life, and we have made this a scientific endeavor rather than a religious one.

Life Before Life is therefore analytical rather than emotional or religious. I will not try to convince you that these cases prove that reincarnation occurs, to promote a theory. Instead, I will present the cases so that you can assess them and reach your own conclusions about what they mean. I will give my analysis of where I think the evidence leads us, but you should also be forming your own opinions along the way. In doing so, you should not be too quick to make a judgment, either that the cases are nonsense or that they are definitive proof of reincarnation. Instead, I would encourage you to take the same analytical approach that we have used in doing the research.

These cases are not about "proof," they are about evidence.

Since this work has taken place in the messy real world rather than a tightly controlled laboratory, proof is not possible. This is often the case in science and medicine. For example, many medications are judged to be helpful, because evidence indicates that they work even though they have not been absolutely proven to do so. Our work also involves an area, the possibility of life after death, that does not easily lend itself to being researched. Some people even say that researchers should not try to study the subject of life after death scientifically since it is so far removed from usual empirical areas of investigation. Nevertheless, there is no bigger question in the world than whether we can survive death, and researchers have attempted to collect the best evidence possible to answer it, evidence that I will share with you.

Each case of course has its unique aspects, but we can discuss typical features found in many of the cases. In later chapters, we will then examine in depth a number of cases that include each of these features.

Predictions, Experimental Birthmarks, and Dreams Before Birth

Sometimes, the case begins before the child, the *subject* of the case, is even born. One situation involves an elderly or dying individual, the *previous personality,* making a prediction about his or her next life. Such cases are rare, but they do occur with some frequency among two groups. One is the lamas of Tibet. Though their predictions can be vague or unclear, others use these predictions to identify young children as the lamas reborn. In the case of the current Dalai Lama, his predecessor apparently did not make any predictions, so other clues such as meditation visions after his death were used to find the boy identified as his rebirth.

The Tlingits, a tribe in Alaska, frequently make predictions about rebirth. Of forty-six cases there, the previous personality made a prediction about his or her subsequent rebirth in ten of them. In eight of the ten, the person gave the names of the parents to which he or she wanted to be reborn. For example, a man named Victor Vincent told his niece that he was going to come back as her son. He showed her two scars he had from minor surgeries and predicted that he would carry those marks to his next life. Eighteen months after he died, she gave birth to a boy who had birthmarks in the same spots. One of them even had small round marks lined up beside the main linear mark, giving the appearance of stitch wounds from a surgical scar. The boy later said that he was the previous personality, and he seemed to recognize several people from Victor's life.

Some cases involve another feature that occurs before the child is born. In several Asian countries, a family member or friend may mark the body of a dying or deceased individual in hopes that when that person is reborn, the baby will have a birthmark that matches the marking. This practice is known as experimental birthmarks, and we will look at it in detail in Chapter 4.

An announcing dream can occur before the birth of the child. With this feature, a family member, usually the subject's mother, has a dream before or during the pregnancy in which the previous personality either announces that he or she is coming to the expecting mother or asks to come to her. Such dreams usually occur in *same-family* cases, ones in which the previous personality is a deceased member of the subject's family, or in cases in which the subject's mother at least knew the previous personality. Exceptions do occur as we will soon see. Cases from all the various cultures have included announcing dreams, which have occurred in approximately 22 percent of the first 1,100 cases in our computer database. They are much more common in some places than others, and they also tend to occur at different times in different places. In Myanmar, families generally report that the dreams occur before the child is conceived, whereas among the tribes in northwest North America, they tend to occur at the very end of the pregnancy.

Birthmarks and Birth Defects

Many of the subjects in our cases are born with birthmarks or birth defects that match wounds on the body of the previous personality, usually fatal wounds. One case that includes both an announcing dream and a birth defect is that of Süleyman Çaper in Turkey. His mother dreamed during her pregnancy that a man she did not recognize told her, "I was killed with a blow from a shovel. I want to stay with you and not anyone else." When Süleyman was born, the back of his skull was partially depressed, and he also had a birthmark there. When he became able to talk, he said that he had been a miller who died when an angry customer hit him on the head. Along with other details, he gave the first name of the miller and the village where he had lived. In fact, an angry customer had killed a miller with that name in that village by hitting him on the back of the head with a shovel.

Many of the birthmarks are not small discolorations. Instead, they are often unusual in shape or size and are often puckered or raised rather than simply being flat. Some can be quite dramatic and unusual in appearance. In Chapter 4, I will discuss the case of Patrick, a boy in Michigan, who had three distinct lesions that matched those of the previous personality. There are several cases in which a small, round birthmark matching a typical bullet entrance wound and a larger, more irregularly shaped birthmark matching a typical exit wound were both present. Other examples include cases with birthmarks in such unusual places as wrapping around an ankle and cases with deformities like missing or malformed limbs or digits.

In these cases, the birthmarks and birth defects can provide a concrete indication of a connection between the subject and the previous personality. Since they remain on the body, birthmarks and defects are not dependent on witnesses' memories to be part of the case. When an autopsy report or a medical record of the previous personality is available, as it was in Süleyman's case, researchers can objectively compare it to the birthmarks to see how well they correspond.

Such birthmarks and birth defects are not rare among our cases. A third of the cases from India include birthmarks or birth defects that are thought to correspond to wounds on the previous personalities, with 18 percent of those including medical records that confirm the match. I should note that the actual percentage of all children reporting past-life memories who have birthmarks might be much lower. We often have to make decisions about which cases to investigate, and since we are particularly interested in the birthmark cases, we are more likely to pursue them than other types of cases. Thus, we end up registering more of them.

Past-life Statements

The key feature in our cases, of course, is the statements that the children make about a past life. As an example, when Suzanne Ghanem of Lebanon was less than a year old, her first word was "Leila," and she would pick up the telephone and say, "Hello, Leila." She began telling her family about a previous life that ended when she went to the United States for heart surgery. She talked about this life a great deal, but her family was not able to track down the previous personality until Suzanne was five years old. At that point, Suzanne met the family of the woman who she thought she had been, and she convinced them that she was the woman reborn when she knew details about that life. The woman, who died at a medical center in the United States after heart surgery, turned out to have a daughter named Leila, who was not able to join her there because of passport problems. Before the woman died, her brother at the hospital tried to telephone Leila for her but was unsuccessful. In all, Suzanne made forty statements about the previous life that were verified as accurate, including the names of twenty-five people.

The children make these statements at a very early age. Most who talk about a past life begin doing so between the ages of two and four. Some parents say that their children made detailed statements about a previous life at a surprisingly young age, but as we will discuss later, psychological testing has now shown that many of these children are very intelligent. The early advanced language skills necessary to make such statements would be consistent with the testing. The children almost always stop talking about the past life around the age of six or seven, and they seem to go on to lead normal lives after that.

During the time that the children are talking about the past life, some do so in a very matter-of-fact manner while others show great emotion. One example of the latter is a boy in Seattle named Joey. He talked a number of times about his other mother dying in a car accident. One night at dinner when he was almost four years old, he stood up in his chair and appeared pale as he looked intently at his mother and said, "You are not my family—my family is dead." He cried quietly for a minute as a tear rolled down his cheek, then sat back down and continued with his meal. The fact that his mother had a dinner guest that night did not help the awkwardness of the situation, though she proved to be quite understanding.

Some children only make a few comments about the past life and only talk about it at certain times, often during relaxed periods, while others talk about it almost constantly and make many statements. In general, the children tend to talk about people and events from near the end of the previous life. A child who describes a past life that ended in adulthood is likely to talk about a spouse or children rather than talking about parents. Seventy-five percent of the children describe the way that they died in their previous life, and the mode of death is frequently violent or sudden.

The lives that the children describe tend to be very recent ones, and in fact, the median time between the death of the previous personality and the birth of the subject is only fifteen to sixteen months. Exceptions certainly exist, as Kemal's case in the Introduction shows, but most of the children describe very recent lives. Few report having been famous personalities, as almost all describe ordinary lives, often ending in very unpleasant ways.

When the children give enough information so that one particular deceased individual can be identified as the previous personality, we say that the case is *solved*. If the previous personality has not been identified, we say that the case is *unsolved*. A colleague told me that he objects to the term "unsolved" in this instance, because it implies that the child is actually remembering the life of one unique previous personality who could be identified if the case could only be solved. This is not what we mean when we use the term. We can all agree that an unsolved case, or a solved one for that matter, does not automatically indicate a case of reincarnation.

With only rare exceptions, almost all of the children describe only one previous life. In addition, though most children do not talk about the time between lives, some occasionally do. Their statements can involve either events that took place on earth, for example the funeral of the previous personality, or descriptions of other realms. An example of the latter is a boy named Kenny who, though his case was unsolved, gave numerous details about the life of a man who died in an automobile accident. He said that after he died, another spirit, probably the driver of the vehicle, took him by the hand, and the two of them were with other spirits in what seemed to be a huge hall. He said another spirit he took to be God told him that there were people wishing for a child and that he had been chosen to go down to be born.

Past-life Behaviors

In addition to the statements, many children show behaviors that seem connected to the past-life memories they are reporting.

Many show strong emotions related to their memories. In some cases, the children cry and beg their parents to take them to their previous family until their parents finally relent. In a case in which the previous personality was murdered, the subject may also display an immense anger toward the killer. I will discuss a case later in which a toddler tried to strangle the man he said had killed him in his previous life.

The children often demonstrate unusual play. For instance, Parmod Sharma in India became wrapped up in his play as a shopkeeper of biscuits and soda water, the occupation of the previous personality, from the ages of four to seven. This caused him to neglect his work when he started school, and he never seemed to fully recover. His mother blamed his poor school performance and subsequent limited vocational opportunities on his preoccupation with his past-life memories and his shopkeeping play as a young child. That case is an extreme example, but the play can be excessive. In these cases, the children repeat the same play over and over, and it is play that is not seen in the other children of the family or modeled after an adult family member or close family friend. Most commonly, the child mimics the occupation of the previous personality as Parmod did, and the drive that some of these children demonstrate in wanting to engage repeatedly in the play can be quite striking. Other children have repeatedly acted out the death scene from the previous life. This can be similar to the post-traumatic play of children who have been through difficult experiences, only in this case the trauma is thought to be from a previous life rather than the current one.

Phobias seem to be linked to the past-life memories at times. Many of the children show intense fear related to the method of the previous personality's death. Often, these fears will show up before the child has begun to report past-life memories. For example, a very young child may show an intense fear of water. As a baby in Sri Lanka, Shamlinie Prema always had to be held down by three adults in order to be bathed, and then later told of having drowned in the previous life.

Some children are also unusually fond of certain things, including foods the previous personality especially enjoyed or even alcohol or tobacco products. Though the use of alcohol and tobacco is common in various cultures, consumption is not considered appropriate for three-year-olds. Parents have been amused and appalled by their children's attempts to get alcohol. As for foods, one particularly prominent example is the request to eat raw fish from Burmese children who say they remember lives as Japanese soldiers.

When unusual play, phobias, and preferences are present along with statements or birthmarks or other features, the impression of a link between the subject and the previous personality is strengthened. Such cases are often about more than possible memories or statements; they suggest that behaviors and emotions have carried over as well.

Past-life Recognitions

Sometimes subjects recognize, or are thought to recognize, people or places from their past lives. Frequently, when the subject's family takes the child to the home of the previous personality, the subject seems to recognize members of the previous family. At times, the previous family is hoping that their deceased loved one has returned, so they may be open to interpreting anything the child does as evidence that he recognizes them. Others are much more skeptical, and some suspect that the subject's family is hoping for financial gain in making the claim, even though this seems rarely to be the case. Some will engineer such informal tests for the child as having him identify objects that belonged to the previous personality before deciding whether to accept the claims.

In a much smaller number of cases, subjects have been tested under more controlled conditions, and we will review some of these in Chapter 7. The strongest examples add to the impression that something is going on that cannot be written off as simply wishful thinking or childhood fantasy.

In summary, cases from all over the world can include birthmarks that match wounds on the previous personality, statements that are accurate for the life of that person, behaviors that appear to be linked to the person—strong emotions, unusual play, phobias, and unusual preferences—and situations in which the child was judged to recognize something or someone from that life.

CHAPTER 2

Investigating the Cases

The story of this research at the University of Virginia begins in 1958. By any standard, Dr. Ian Stevenson had achieved a successful academic career at that point. After graduating at the top of his medical school class at McGill University, he had initially studied biochemistry before becoming interested in psychosomatic medicine, the study of the connections between emotions and health. He had written extensively, almost always in medical journals but several times also in *Harper's Magazine* and *The New Republic,* and by 1958, he had seventy publications to his credit. A year earlier, he had become the chairman of the Department of Psychiatry at the University of Virginia at the unusually young age of thirty-eight.

Along with these accomplishments, Dr. Stevenson was interested in paranormal phenomena—ones beyond current scientific explanation. When the American Society for Psychical Research announced a contest in 1958 for the best essay on paranormal mental phenomena and their relationship to life after death, he submitted the winning entry, entitled, "The Evidence for Survival from Claimed Memories of Former Incarnations." In this essay, he reviewed forty-four cases that had previously been published of individuals from various parts of the world who had described memories of previous lives. The reports came from a number of sources—books, magazines, and newspapers. Almost all of the most impressive cases involved children who were under the age of ten when they first reported the memories, and in many of them, the children were three years old or younger. Dr. Stevenson was struck by the pattern of children from very different places making similar statements about past-life memories. As he said later, "These forty-four cases, when you put them together, it just seemed inescapable to me that there must be something there." He ended the paper by saying that the evidence he presented did not permit any definite conclusion about reincarnation, but he felt that more extensive study was justified.

After the paper was published in 1960, Dr. Stevenson began to hear about new cases. After learning of four or five cases in India and one in Ceylon (now Sri Lanka), he took a trip to investigate. Once he got to India, he was surprised by how many cases he found. In four weeks, he investigated twenty-five cases. Likewise, he visited Ceylon for one week and found five or six cases. He concluded that children reported memories of previous lives much more frequently than anyone had previously known.

One person who read Dr. Stevenson's essay was Chester Carlson, the inventor of the photocopying process that formed the basis for the Xerox Corporation. His wife, Dorris Carlson, had gotten him interested in parapsychology. After reading the essay, he contacted Dr. Stevenson to offer financial support. Dr. Stevenson initially declined the offer, because he was busy with his other work, but as he collected more cases and became increasingly intrigued by what he found, he accepted funding support from Carlson.

In 1966, he published his first book on the topic, *Twenty Cases*

Suggestive of Reincarnation. Dr. Stevenson had worked hard to verify independently what the twenty children had said and how well their statements matched the lives of the individuals the children were thought to remember. The book consisted of very detailed reports of cases from India, Ceylon, Brazil, and Lebanon that included lists of every person Dr. Stevenson interviewed about each case, along with lengthy tables in which each of the child's statements about a previous life was listed along with the informant for that statement and the person or persons who had verified that the statement was correct for the life of the deceased individual. Dr. Stevenson presented the cases in an objective, evenhanded manner, and he discussed their weaknesses as well as their strengths.

A number of journals, including the prestigious *American Journal of Psychiatry,* gave the book positive reviews, with reviewers often noting Dr. Stevenson's painstaking work and objectivity, and it has continued to be well regarded over the years because of those features.

With the help of assistants, Dr. Stevenson was soon finding cases in a number of countries, and he made trips to India, Sri Lanka, Turkey, Lebanon, Thailand, Burma, Nigeria, Brazil, and Alaska. After publishing *Twenty Cases,* he also began to learn of occasional cases in this country.

With Carlson's funding, Dr. Stevenson was able to step down as chairman of the Department of Psychiatry in 1967 to focus full-time on his research. The dean of the medical school, who did not approve of the work, was happy to see Dr. Stevenson step down, and he agreed to allow the formation of a small research division, now known as the Division of Personality Studies, where the work would take place.

The following year, Chester Carlson died suddenly of a heart attack. Since the division was dependent on Mr. Carlson's funding in order to operate, Dr. Stevenson assumed that he would have to try a return to more routine research. Carlson's will was then opened, and he had left one million dollars to the University of Virginia for Dr. Stevenson's work.

At that point, controversy broke out regarding whether the university would accept the money, given the unusual nature of the research. Universities are not in the habit of turning down million-dollar gifts, but the situation clearly made some people uneasy. The university eventually did decide to accept the money since it had been given to support scholarly work, and the work continued.

Dr. Stevenson wrote more books about the cases, and these continued to be well received by at least some in the field. In reviewing one, Lester S. King, the Book Review Editor of *JAMA: The Journal of the American Medical Association,* wrote that "in regard to reincarnation [Stevenson] has painstakingly and unemotionally collected a detailed series of cases from India, cases in which the evidence is difficult to explain on any other grounds." He also added, "He has placed on record a large amount of data that cannot be ignored."

In 1977, the *Journal of Nervous and Mental Disease* devoted most of one issue to Dr. Stevenson's reincarnation work. It included a paper by Dr. Stevenson and commentaries on it from several others. Dr. Harold Lief, a well-respected figure in the field of psychiatry, wrote one of the commentaries. He described Dr. Stevenson as "a methodical, careful, even cautious, investigator, whose personality is on the obsessive side." He also wrote, "Either he is making a colossal mistake, or he will be known . . . as 'the Galileo of the twentieth century.' "

Dr. Stevenson gradually got others interested in investigating cases. Satwant Pasricha, a psychologist in India, began assisting Dr. Stevenson on the cases there, and she continues to research them today. Erlendur Haraldsson, a psychologist at the University of Iceland who had a long history in experimental psychology, became interested in the cases in the 1970s, and he has studied them ever since. Antonia Mills, an anthropologist who received her Ph.D. from Harvard, began assisting Dr. Stevenson on cases in northwest North America, and she has since investigated cases independently there and in India. Jürgen Keil, who investigated Kemal's case in the Introduction, is a psychologist at the University of Tasmania who was able to establish new contacts in Turkey, Thailand, and Myanmar in order to study cases in those locations. In addition, he and I made two trips to Thailand and Myanmar to study cases together, and I will be describing some of those later in the book. Dr. Stevenson investigated most of the cases from Asia that I will discuss, and the end notes at the back of the book list the references for his detailed reports of the cases.

He became particularly interested in cases in which a child was born with a birthmark that matched a wound on the deceased individual. He believes in strength in numbers, so he held off publishing any of these cases until he could publish a series of them in a book. After several delays, he published *Reincarnation and Biology: A Contribution to the Etiology of Birthmarks and Birth Defects* in 1997. The work is massive—2,200 pages long in two volumes—and it includes detailed reports of 225 cases along with pictures of the various birthmarks. Dr. Stevenson published it as he approached his eightieth birthday. Though *Reincarnation and Biology* in some ways represented the culmination of his decades of work, he was still not done and continued to write and research cases.

I came onto the scene in 1996, and I eventually left my private practice in psychiatry to pursue this research. Recently, I have been focusing on American cases. Though they are harder to find here, American cases occur without the cultural factors that some critics hold responsible for cases in other parts of the world. I will use a number of these American cases to illustrate the various aspects of the experiences. When I do, I will change the names of the children and other identifying details. I will do so for the international cases as well unless a case report has already been published that used the child's real name.

As for Dr. Stevenson, he has continued to show enthusiasm for the work. He retired in 2002, perhaps with a reluctance that few people in their eighties would feel toward retirement, partly to focus more on his writings but also to spend more time with his wife, Margaret. He had talked about cutting back on the research trips for years but had failed to do so. Even after he retired, he took one final "final trip" to India. Margaret once said that she did not mind his taking the trips, but she wished that he would stop referring to each one as the last. He wrote yet another book in 2003—*European Cases of the Reincarnation Type*—and continued to work on other papers and book projects. His publications now number more than 290.

The Investigations

Before we investigate cases, we have to find them. We have done so wherever we have looked for them, but cases are easiest to find in areas with a general belief in reincarnation. This includes India and Sri Lanka, where Dr. Stevenson made his initial trips, along with other countries with similar beliefs, including Thailand, Myanmar (Burma), Turkey, and among the Druses in Lebanon. The geographical pattern of cases is determined to some extent by where we have people looking for them. We have been fortunate to have assistants in each of these countries looking for cases for us. They find them through a variety of means, some from occasional newspaper articles but most through word of mouth. We go where they find them. That does not mean, of course, that cases do not occur in areas where we are not looking for them. We have many cases from Thailand but essentially none from Vietnam, and this may simply be because we have no connection in Vietnam.

In fact, we have found cases on all the continents except for Antarctica, and no one has looked for them there. In some ways, looking for cases here in the United States is harder than in other countries. In Thailand, we sometimes seem to hit areas where we cannot stop to ask for directions without hearing about another case. In the United States, on the other hand, we cannot just walk into a convenience store and ask if anyone knows of a child talking about a past life. That does not mean that the cases are not here. When I give talks, people often speak to me afterwards to mention a family member who at one point talked about a past life. Since we set up our Web site in 1998, www.healthsystem.virginia.edu/personalitystudies, we have received e-mails from dozens of American families describing a child who reported past-life memories.

We tend to use the same general methods when we investigate a case. We usually conduct the interviews through a translator, since few of the families in the international cases speak English. Though this may introduce a potential source for error in the process, the native translators are able to understand the informants with ease. We often clarify any potential misunderstandings with the translator until we are sure that we have understood what the informants are trying to tell us. After working with us a while, our translators come to understand what we are trying to learn in the interviews, and they are careful to ask whatever questions are necessary to gather a clear understanding of the events that have taken place. All of this means that the interviews sometimes proceed very slowly, with us repeatedly making sure that we understand exactly what has happened, but the families usually tolerate us quite well. We never pay them, since doing so could lead people to make up cases, but they are almost always hospitable during our visits.

Most of the time, we get to a case after it has been solved. This means that the child gave enough details about the previous life to enable the family to find and meet the family of the previous personality. This meeting has occurred a few weeks before our arrival in some cases and years before in others. Sometimes, the case is unsolved when we arrive, and the two families have not met. Though this is obviously our preference, it is most often not the case, and our job becomes an effort to reconstruct as accurately as possible what was said and done in the case before we got there.

We usually start our investigation by interviewing the subject's family. We begin all the interviews by explaining the research so that all those involved can agree to participate in it. We then start out with general open-ended questions about the history of a case. This interview is usually with the parents of the subject, but grandparents or other family members can participate as well. We do not begin with the subjects. Often, they have little or nothing to say about the case. If they are quite young, they may be too shy to talk with us, or they may not be in the right frame of mind to discuss the case. If they are older, they may not remember anything about the case. We attempt to talk to them, but we place the greatest emphasis on what the adults can tell us about the child's statements or behaviors when the case was beginning. If the family has met the family of the previous personality, we are most interested in what the subject said before the two families met, since his or her statements after the families met could be colored by information learned from the previous personality's family.

If the case involves a birthmark, then obviously we ask to see the birthmark on the child. We then photograph it and note its location and appearance on a human figure drawing, since our photography at times can lead to disappointing results. The parents sometimes say that the birthmark moved as the child grew older, so we note their description of the location of the mark when the child was born.

Some children only tell their parents about their memories, but others tell any number of people. In the latter situation, we attempt to interview as many additional witnesses as possible. What we do not accept is hearsay testimony. If a villager says that he or she heard that the subject made a certain statement, we do not accept it unless we can talk with someone who actually heard the child firsthand.

After we get as much information as possible from the subject's side of the case, we move to the previous personality's side. We talk to the family members to verify how closely the child's statements matched the life of the previous personality. We also find out their impressions of their first meeting with the child.

Since the child is often said to recognize members of the previous personality's family or belongings of the previous personality at this meeting, we want to get the testimony of both families about it.

When Dr. Stevenson has published reports of cases in his books, he has included a list of all the statements that each child has made about a previous life. Each statement is then followed by the name of the informant who heard the statement, whether the statement was verified as accurate for the previous personality and if so by whom, and any additional comments. By seeing all the statements, the correct ones as well as the incorrect ones, readers are able to judge the cases in their entirety without worrying that the child may have had one or two lucky hits in a sea of misses.

In addition to the statements, other aspects of the cases often need to be investigated as well. When the child has a birthmark that is thought to match a wound on the body of the deceased, we then attempt to determine how close that match actually is. In the best of circumstances, an autopsy report exists that records the wounds on the body of the previous personality. If the birthmark matches a nonfatal wound on the previous personality, then medical records may also be helpful in assessing the match. In the case of a violent death, a police record may be available even if an autopsy record is not, and it may document wounds.

Since no written record of any kind is available that documents the wounds in the case of many of these villagers, eyewitness testimony then becomes the best evidence available. Family members have often seen the body of the previous personality at death or have helped prepare the body for funeral. A number of people may have noticed wounds, and we try to talk to them so that we can be as sure as possible about what wounds were present and where they were located. Dr. Keil and I published a case in which the subject's family thought that the birth defects on his hands corresponded to wounds that the previous personality suffered during a fatal parachuting accident. Through persistent effort, Dr. Keil eventually determined with some certainty that the previous personality did not actually have any major wounds on his hands.

In many cases, the investigators have conducted follow-up interviews in subsequent trips to the area. This serves several purposes. One obviously is to learn if any new developments have occurred in the case. Another is to find out if the testimony of the witnesses stays consistent over time. Lastly, the subject's subsequent life and development can be assessed. Dr. Stevenson has followed some cases for decades, so he has seen the subjects grow up.

After a case is investigated, it is registered in our files at the university if it meets certain criteria. These involve many of the features we have discussed, and according to the criteria, a case has to have at least two of the following:

1. Prediction of rebirth—not just "I will be reborn" but with some specifying details; for example, selection of next parents
2. An announcing dream
3. Birthmarks or birth defects related to previous life—not just any nevus or other blemish; also the birthmark/birth defect should be noticed immediately after birth or within a few weeks
4. Statements by the subject, as a child, about a previous life—the record of these should not depend on the

subject alone: at least one other older person (for example, a parent or older sibling) should corroborate that the subject spoke about a previous life as a child

5. Recognitions by subject of persons or objects with which the previous personality was familiar
6. Unusual behavior on the part of the subject—that is, behavior that is unusual in subject's family and that apparently corresponds to similar behavior shown by the presumed previous personality or that could be conjectured for him/her (for example, a phobia of firearms if the previous personality was fatally shot)

No criteria are perfect in all situations. One concern I have is that a case could have enough impressive statements by the child so that we would want to include it even if none of the other features were present. Other situations could certainly arise in which a case would meet these criteria, but we would choose not to include it in the collection. Overall, these criteria have served us well, and I hope they make clear what is required for us to include a case in our series.

These criteria show that a wide diversity in the strength of cases can exist. Some cases offer compelling evidence that something unusual has happened, while the evidence is far less convincing in others. The strength of these cases often lies in the eye of the beholder, but we think that collecting as many as possible is important so that the beholder has the best information on which to base a judgment.

With each case, the investigators fill out a registration form, which is an eight-page form that asks for various details about each case. The file also includes notes of the various interviews along with any photographs or records that have been obtained. At some point, all of this information is then transferred onto a coding form so that it can be entered into a computer database. It includes 200 variables that are assigned values that can then be entered into the computer. These range from the subject's country of origin to the parents' initial reactions to the child's statements, the distance between the subject's family and the previous family, and dozens of other minute details. By entering such information into a database, we can see features of the cases as a group that we cannot observe from just the individual cases. For instance, when I said that 18 percent of the Indian birthmark cases include medical records that confirm the match, I knew this because we have all 421 Indian cases entered into the computer, and I can simply look at the frequencies for that item. This process is labor intensive, and getting all the cases into the database is years away. At this point, we have entered 1,100 out of the 2,500 cases into the computer database. It includes all the Indian cases but as yet includes virtually no cases from Thailand and Myanmar, even though those two countries have combined to produce hundreds of cases. I will give figures from time to time based on these 1,100 cases, but we should remember that these are not necessarily representative of all 2,500 cases. As we get more cases coded during the next few years, we can expect to learn more about the phenomenon, even about the cases that researchers investigated years ago.

CHAPTER 3

Explanations to Consider

Abby Swanson, a young girl who lives in Ohio, was four years old when she began talking to her mother one night after having her bath. "Mommy, I used to give you baths when you were a baby," she said. "Oh really?" her mom replied. "Uh huh. You cried," Abby responded. "I did?" said her mom. "Yep," Abby said. "I was your grandma."

"And what was your name?" her mother asked her. She remembers her hair standing on end as Abby considered the question, tapping her mouth with her fingers.

"Lucy? . . . Ruthie? . . . Ruthie," she finally said. Since this was Abby's great-grandmother's name, her mother tried to ask her more questions, but Abby did not say anything else.

Abby's great-grandmother died in 1985, nine years before Abby was born. She had twenty grandchildren, and unlike most of the others, Abby's mother lived nearby and was close to her while growing up. They had some conflict when Abby's mother was a teenager but then got along well when she became an adult.

Abby's mother would occasionally mention Abby's great-grandparents to her children, but never by name, and she had not talked about them for at least six months before that night. In addition, Abby's grandmother lived on the West Coast and could not have been a source of information for Abby to learn about her great-grandmother. Later, her mother did check with Abby's grandmother to confirm that Abby's great-grandmother had in fact given her mother baths. Abby's grandmother also said that her mother cried a lot when she was given baths as a baby.

Abby's mother is certain that Abby had never heard her great-grandmother's name. In fact, when she asked her a few days later what the name was, Abby did not know. Whatever knowledge, or memory, was available to Abby that night was not available to her after that.

What are we to make of this? Much stronger cases exist, as we will see, but Abby's is a succinct one that we can use to explore the possible explanations for cases of children who report past-life memories. We approach the cases with an attitude of scientific curiosity. Our job is to explore this phenomenon and to try to determine the most likely explanation for each case. In particular, the question of whether or not a case represents a paranormal event—one that is beyond current scientific explanation—is always present and in many regards is the most important question in our work. This question is often impossible to answer. A child may claim to remember a previous life but does not give any information about that life that he or she could not have learned through normal means. In such a case, we cannot say that the child is the reincarnation of the person whose life he or she claims to remember. At the same time, we cannot say with certainty that the child's statements are false, even if we conclude that no evidence exists to support them.

We approach each case with an attitude of wanting to learn as much about it as possible. We do not approach a case with our minds already made up about it. We are open to all possibilities, including that a paranormal link may exist between the child and a deceased individual or that a link may not exist.

This attitude is necessary for scientific inquiry, which is different from the two extremes. On one end, believers in reincarnation may be quick to accept any claim of rebirth that supports their firmly held beliefs. On the other end, individuals convinced that the material universe is all that can possibly exist—including so-called "professional skeptics"—will dismiss any claim that challenges their views. Though many people in scientific fields hold views that can be just as dogmatic as those of an intensely religious person, judging from firmly held beliefs does not make for sound scientific inquiry.

Therefore, we are open to all possibilities. This means that when a child claims to remember a previous life, we think that he or she may be telling the truth. On the other hand, the child may be engaging in fantasy, or the adults may have misinterpreted the child's statements. We are trying to determine what scenario is most likely. Though this is our attitude, I will not, in writing this book, always say that the past-life memories of a child are "alleged" or "claimed." This would be cumbersome and irritating to writer and reader both, and unnecessary, since I have already been explicit about our approach to the cases. I could put "past-life memories" in quotation marks every time I use the term, but that would grow tiresome as well.

I will speculate at times about what a situation might mean if the memories are in fact past-life ones. Though this does not mean that I have concluded that the memories are actually memories of past lives, I do not want us to avoid intriguing areas of interest because we do not yet have final proof of one possibility or another.

As for the possible explanations, there are two basic types. Cases are caused either by a normal process or by a paranormal one. The following list touches on a variety of explanations we should consider.

Normal Explanations

FRAUD

This would mean that Abby's mother intentionally lied to us about what happened. This is theoretically possible. Abby did not remember that night when we met her two years later, and no other witnesses were there to confirm the story. Someone could make up such a story if she had a reason to do so, which is why we only report cases in which we have interviewed the families ourselves. When we interview them, we try to judge how reliable they are.

The problem with the explanation of fraud is that for the vast majority of the cases, the family has absolutely no reason to make up such a story. Abby's mother certainly did not. The only thing that she got out of contacting us was having her home invaded by a psychiatrist and psychologist who asked a lot of questions, so unless she was badly in need of attention from two strangers, she would have no motivation to lie to us. Though she believed in reincarnation, her husband did not. He did not seem thrilled to have us in his home, so any potential unhappiness on his part would have presumably made her even less likely to invent a story when she contacted us. Similarly, the people involved in the cases in other countries get no material benefit. Though families have on rare occasion tried to get gifts from the families of the previous personality, almost all of them have appeared to be ordinary, decent people who happened to have children who said some extraordinary things.

In addition, Abby's case is unusual because there is only one witness. In many of the others, numerous family members and friends have heard the child talk about a previous life, along with several family members of the previous personality who later heard the child as well. For fraud to exist, a conspiracy would have to be responsible, and though the cases may bring the families some brief notoriety, the absence of any meaningful benefit to all the people who would have to be involved in this elaborate undertaking makes this scenario very unlikely.

The other possibility for fraud is that the investigators have made up the cases. We know that we have met these children, but you do not. Nonetheless, the field notes packed in the file cabinets in our offices document that the interviews have taken place. In addition, anyone who reads Dr. Stevenson's write-ups of the cases, in which he highlights the weaknesses of the cases along with the strengths, will understand that he has not committed fraud, even if he is mistaken about the significance of these cases. Another practical objection to investigator fraud is that six of us have published cases, so the fraud would have to involve a number of professionals who have never shown any tendencies toward dishonesty in their work.

Though the possibility exists that Abby's mother made up this story, the chances that fraud is responsible for this case, and for the cases as a group, are quite small.

FANTASY

In this scenario, Abby made up a story when she said that she remembered giving her mother baths. We need to consider this possibility in cases in which the child's statements are unverified, meaning that the cases are unsolved. In many of our American cases, the children have talked a lot about when they lived before, but since they have not given any names, their statements remain unverified. We might think that a young child fantasizing in this way is odd, particularly if the parents dislike the idea of reincarnation, and even odder if the child becomes emotionally wrapped up in the stories, but unless the child demonstrates knowledge that can be verified as accurate, fantasy cannot be ruled out.

Of course, many of these children, including Abby, seem to have shown knowledge that they could not have acquired through normal means, so coincidence is then added to fantasy as part of the explanation. In Abby's case, this would mean that she came up with her great-grandmother's name purely by chance. She did need two tries to get the right name, doubling her chances of success, but considering all the possible names that she could have said, even doubling the chances still makes the odds of successfully picking the correct one quite a long shot.

Proponents of coincidence would say "Not so fast." They argue that we are fooled about how unlikely an event is unless we consider the number of tries it takes to produce it. In this case, the idea that Abby could have correctly guessed her great-grandmother's name seems incredible, but we only heard about the case because she came up with the correct name. A million-to-one shot only seems amazing if you do not know that a million other shots took place along with the successful one. As an example, the fact that anyone ever wins the lottery may seem incredible, given the long odds of winning, but people win every week because so many people are playing. If the odds are twenty million to one and over twenty million people are playing, we should not be surprised when someone wins.

The odds of guessing a name correctly are clearly better than that, since hundreds of names exist but not millions, but this argument runs into serious trouble when we see its eventual conclusion: hundreds of American children have told their parents that they were their great-grandmothers, but the only family that our group heard from was Abby's, because the others came up with an incorrect name. That may be happening all across America, but such a possibility seems preposterous.

Then there is the case of Suzanne Ghanem that I mentioned in Chapter 1. She accurately gave the names of twenty-five people from the previous life and their relationship to the previous personality, while giving only one incorrect name. The odds of her getting that many right by coincidence are so small as to approach zero unless we think that there are millions of children who give twenty-five proper names in describing past lives to their parents, and Suzanne just happened to be the one who was lucky enough to give the correct ones.

Cases with proper names make the coincidence argument seem absurd, but some cases clearly might be due to coincidence. If a child gives general statements about a life but does not give a location, the number of potential matches would be very high, and a deceased individual might be found whose life was similar to the one described by the child simply by coincidence. Even if the child does give a location, coincidence could be a possibility if there are few details given. If a child says, "I was a man who died in California," then a lot of individuals would obviously fit that description.

As we will see, these cases involve a lot more detail than that.

KNOWLEDGE ACQUIRED THROUGH NORMAL MEANS

In this explanation, the child has learned the information about the previous life through normal means but has simply forgotten the source of that information. So, in Abby's case, this means that she heard her great-grandmother's name at some point, later forgot that event, as her mother did, but did not forget the name. This argument has a certain logic. We often know facts but do not remember when we learned them. In this case, her mother was certain that Abby had not heard her great-grandmother's name, and she was too young to have read it in any family document. The idea that she would know the name of her great-grandmother who died nine years before she was born does seem unlikely. Most four-year-olds do not know the names of their deceased great-grandmothers, and a lot of us do not even know them as adults.

Compared to cases involving strangers, the possibility of knowledge being acquired through normal means is greater in cases like Abby's in which the child and the previous personality are in the same family. Being certain that the child has not overheard something about the previous personality can be difficult. Even if Abby had heard her great-grandmother's name at some point, this scenario does not explain why she later thought she had been her great-grandmother and why she developed the memory of giving her mother baths. We know that young children engage in fantasy play, but that would be an unusual game of make-believe.

More importantly, we have to explain the cases in which children have given many specific details about deceased individuals who lived many miles away. Often in those cases, the children appear to have had no possible opportunity to learn the information. On top of that, we must then try to imagine what could have possessed them to think that they had been these strangers in a previous life.

In Abby's case, this scenario is unlikely but possible, since she could have heard her great-grandmother's name at some point, despite her mother's certainty that she had not, but it is essentially impossible for many other cases.

FAULTY MEMORY BY INFORMANTS

Abby's mother might have remembered the conversation she had with Abby that night incorrectly. Arguing against this is the fact that as she waited to hear Abby's response to her question about the great-grandmother's name, her mother knew its significance. This was not something that occurred unexpectedly while she was under great duress, as is the case for witnesses at crime scenes, whose testimony we still use to convict people even if we recognize that eyewitness reports in those circumstances can be imperfect. Her mother waited with great anticipation to hear if Abby could give evidence that confirmed the past-life claim she had just made, increasing her chances of remembering it correctly.

This possibility of faulty memory by informants is the most likely normal explanation for many of our cases, since we often have not gotten to the Asian cases until well after the events in question. Numerous cases have been found in which the family made the following report: The child gave a number of specific details about a past life, including the name of the village in which the previous personality lived. The family then went to the village with the child, who recognized members of the previous family or items belonging to the previous personality. In some cases, the child was also able to give a detail about a person or the location of a particular item that only one or two people knew.

Critics have said that the families must have remembered the events incorrectly. The argument goes like this: A child in a culture with a belief in reincarnation fantasizes about having had a previous life and tells the family about it. The parents, in their eagerness to confirm the existence of the past life, find another family with a deceased individual whose life shared some general features with those reported by the child. The two families then meet and share information. They become convinced that the deceased individual has been reborn, and they tell others about it. When a researcher eventually comes to investigate the case, both families credit the child with giving far more details about the previous individual than he or she actually did.

This possibility exists because the villagers involved generally make no written records of what the child has said, and the investigators often get to a case only after the two families have met. A number of exceptions to this have been documented; for example, the case in India of Bishen Chand Kapoor. The initial investigator of that case made notes of what the boy had said before the case was solved, and his statements included the name of the previous personality's father (though the boy referred to him as his uncle), his caste, the city where he lived (thirty miles away from the boy's home), the facts that he was unmarried, had attended the

Government High School near a river up to the sixth class, and knew Urdu, Hindi, and English, a description of his house as a two-story building with a shrine room and separate apartments for men and women, his great fondness for wine, rohu fish, and dancing girls, and the name of a neighbor, Sunder Lal, who had a house with a green gate. All of those statements were correct, but the boy gave the wrong age for the previous personality at his death (he said twenty when the man died at age thirty-two) and the wrong name of the quarter of the city where the man had lived. When he was taken to that city, he identified the previous personality and his father in an old photograph and also recognized seven places there. He was even able to identify the room in which the previous personality's father had hidden some gold coins that were only found after the boy gave the location.

In all, written records have been made in more than thirty cases before the previous personality was identified, and we will discuss several of them in the upcoming chapters. This number is barely more than 1 percent of the 2,500 cases that have been collected. Does the faulty memory scenario mean that we should disregard the other 99 percent of the cases?

As I mentioned earlier, we know that human memory is not infallible, but that does not mean that it is worthless. To the contrary, we place great value on memory in many situations. Aspects of these cases argue for giving it value here. These children often do not tell their parents about a previous life just once, as Abby did, but repeat their claims again and again. The parents sometimes take the child to the previous place because the child has worn them down with repeated requests to go there. The parents have had numerous opportunities to learn exactly what the child is claiming before they ever meet the other family.

In many of the cases, multiple witnesses have heard what the children said about the previous life before the two families met, since they talked about their memories emphatically for several years. A number of people would have to have faulty memories about the children's statements for the scenario of faulty memory of informants to be accurate.

We should also note that in a case involving strangers, the child has to give enough details for the parents to identify a family with a deceased member whose life matched the statements. This often means names of people or places or a substantial number of details. Even if the families have imperfect memories about the child's statements before the families met, those statements would have to include a number of discriminating ones.

Other cases exist in which the faulty memory explanation is largely irrelevant: those with written records of the statements that were recorded before the two families met, for example. Also the birthmark and birth defect cases, in which autopsy reports confirm that the child was born with a mark or defect that corresponds to a wound suffered by the previous personality, clearly do not involve faulty memory.

Even without those features, the other components that many of our cases show are important to remember. Intense emotional longing for the previous family, long-standing phobias related to the mode of death of the previous personality, and unusual preferences can be part of these cases, and they are not dependent on the families' memories of particular statements. Since Abby's case does not have any of these characteristics, the faulty memory by informants possibility is more likely here than it is in many of the other cases. On the other hand, Abby's case, along with the dozens of others like it from the United States, shows that children can talk about previous lives even in cultures without a belief in reincarnation. This undercuts the premise of the faulty memory argument that the Asian cultures help create the cases there because of the predominant belief in reincarnation. Though we should keep in mind that her mother's belief in reincarnation could have affected Abby, we have the question of what would make children in America, many of whom have parents who do not believe in reincarnation, think that they have been reincarnated. And what do we make of the fact that not only did Abby think she had been reincarnated, but she also came up with information from a previous life?

If we think that Abby's mother had faulty memory, we have to assume that the families of other nearly identical American cases did as well. I recently corresponded with a mother whose two-and-a-half-year-old daughter told her one day, "I'm your mom. I'm your mom, Debbie." The mother did not think that she had ever mentioned her own mother, who had been dead for twenty-five years, to her toddler daughter, and certainly not by her first name. In another case, a girl, when she was between two and a half and three years old, said to her mother, "I was your grandma, and I couldn't walk." Her family said that the girl had never been told that her great-grandmother had been unable to walk on account of polio. In a fourth case, a three-year-old girl made a number of statements about being her great-grandmother, including telling her grandmother, who was adopted at the age of three, "You were just little like I am now, and you came to live with me at my house." Her grandmother was stunned, as were the witnesses in these other cases. Can we think that they all had faulty memory about these very distinctive statements?

GENETIC MEMORY

This explanation, included here only for the sake of completeness, bridges the two categories of explanations, those of normal means and those of paranormal means, because it involves a "normal" process that is not accepted in mainstream medical thought. Genetic memory is the concept that knowledge people acquire can be transmitted through their genes to their offspring. How information could change the genetic structure in an individual's cells is unknown, and most people in medicine do not believe it is possible. Even if we grant that such a transmission could be possible, the obvious problem with genetic memory as an explanation for these cases is that, in many of them, the child is not related to the previous personality. Some people might think that we are all distantly related in some way, but here the child would have to be not only related but a direct descendent of the previous personality in order to have gotten any of the memories that existed in that person's genes. That is not the situation in many of our cases, so genetic memory does not provide an explanation for them. In Abby's case, of course, she is a direct descendent of her great-grandmother, but since her great-grandmother's memory of bathing her mother came after she had produced her offspring, those memories could not have been included in the genes that Abby eventually received.

Paranormal Explanations

Since paranormal means something that is beyond normal scientific explanation, some readers may view all such scenarios as absurd. Those readers are probably not aware of the volume of research that has been done in parapsychology, which I will not review here. If we are going to consider reincarnation as a possible explanation for these cases, we might as well consider other paranormal possibilities as well.

EXTRASENSORY PERCEPTION (ESP)

As the name states, ESP involves perception by means other than the physical senses, and several types have been described. With *telepathy,* one person gains knowledge from the mind of another person through paranormal means. In Abby's case, this would mean that she read her mother's mind when she came up with her great-grandmother's name. Another type is *clairvoyance,* in which a person gains knowledge in a paranormal way without learning it from another person's mind. For instance, a person who can give details about people after handling such objects as their car keys is a clairvoyant if those details could not have been deduced from the appearance of the objects.

The concept of *superpsi* holds that individuals, through ESP or psi, as it is also called, can essentially know anything that is possible to know. This means that Abby could have known her great-grandmother's name, even if her mother did not, as long as someone somewhere knew the name, whether they were thinking of it at the time or not. For that matter, she could have known it even if no one alive knew it as long as it was written down somewhere for her to learn through clairvoyance. This concept argues that ESP is powerful enough to explain all evidence that suggests survival after bodily death. If a medium tells someone that their deceased Aunt Suzy says there is a box of money buried underneath a particular tree in the backyard, and the person then digs up such a box, the superpsi hypothesis would say that the medium gained the knowledge through clairvoyance about the box and not by speaking with the spirit of Aunt Suzy. Any knowledge that can be later verified could have been available to an individual through superpsi.

One problem with the idea of superpsi is that it is so broad that it can be used to explain anything. Since superpsi could be responsible for anything that anyone might know, the hypothesis cannot be disproved in a test, meaning that it cannot be proved in a test either.

Even if one does accept the possibility of telepathy, clairvoyance, or superpsi, the ESP explanation, like many of those in the normal group, can only account for part of a case. It might explain how Abby was able to come up with her great-grandmother's name, but it would not explain why she thought she had been her great-grandmother. The sense of identification that is so strong in many of these cases is more than just paranormal knowledge; it represents a sense of having been another person. The knowledge that the children express about the previous lives comes from the vantage point of one individual, the previous personality.

The ESP explanation also does not explain the birthmark cases. When we consider the 225 cases in *Reincarnation and Biology* in which the subject of the case had a birthmark or birth defect that matched a wound on the deceased individual, we need another, separate explanation for the birthmarks if we decide that those children's statements were due to ESP.

Along with these problems is the fact that, with very rare exceptions, these children never demonstrate any other paranormal abilities. Abby certainly did not. These children are not young mystics waiting to grow up to be professional psychics; they are children who develop normally, just like their peers.

In Abby's case, she was a four-year-old child without any paranormal ability who gave her great-grandmother's name after describing a memory from her life. Her impression of having been her great-grandmother did not grow from her knowledge of the name. Instead, her ability to give the name came after she seemed to remember a part of that life. This makes ESP a weak and incomplete explanation for the case.

POSSESSION

This refers to the idea that a spirit has inhabited the body and mind of an individual. When many people hear the term possession, they think of evil spirits taking over someone's body, as in the movie *The Exorcist.* It can refer to more benign ideas as well, such as the spirit of a deceased individual, without a body of its own, coming to inhabit the body of someone else. As such, the main difference between possession and reincarnation would be when the spirit came to inhabit the body. If the spirit of the deceased individual entered the new body before birth, then that would be no different from reincarnation unless it forced another spirit out of the body. For all we know, spirits may fight over new bodies routinely.

Possession would be worth considering in situations in which a person underwent a major personality change, developed memories of the previous life, and lost memories of past events of the current life. That is not the case with these children and certainly not the case with Abby. She seemed briefly to have a glimmer of a distant memory, and this is far different from having her mind and body taken over by the spirit of her great-grandmother. In cases with more memories and statements, the families do not report that major changes in personality or skills occur when the statements begin. Instead, some features of the cases, for example, phobias related to the cause of death of the previous personality, often come well before the children start talking about a previous life.

REINCARNATION

We are now down to the last possibility: reincarnation, the concept of an individual dying and then being reborn into another body. In this scenario, when Abby's great-grandmother died, her consciousness did not cease to exist. Instead, it was reborn as part of Abby, who later had some memories of the previous life.

This idea fits with what Abby thought she remembered, giving her mother baths when her mother was a baby and being her mother's grandmother. There are, at most, two people who could have remembered doing both, and one of them was named Ruthie. This explanation does not reveal where she was in the intervening years or how she ended up as Abby, but it does seem to fit the facts of the case better than the ESP and possession explanations do.

The reincarnation idea does not explain why this memory was so fleeting for Abby. In other cases, some of the children only talk about the memories at certain times, while some seem to have access to them at all times during their early years. Perhaps we should not be surprised that memory varies. Some people remember virtually nothing about their childhoods, while others remember voluminous amounts. Sometimes, things happen that trigger a memory that we had not thought of for many years. We also have memories from the very distant past that can be hard to grasp fully at times. We have a vague sense of them that may become stronger if we focus on them. This situation can be similar to remembering dreams. We remember some dreams when we first wake up, but then they disappear, sometimes almost instantly. The memory was there, and then it was gone. So this memory appears to have been for Abby.

Of course, given how remarkable the idea seems that a child could remember a previous life at all, perhaps we should not gripe that the memory was so short-lived. When we look at the whole group of cases, we will see that many of the children had similar memories for at least several years.

One advantage of the idea of reincarnation is that it provides an explanation for the various parts of the cases. The identification with the previous personality is present because the children were, in fact, the previous personalities in the prior lifetime. The memories were simply carried over by the surviving consciousness into the new life. The birthmarks reflect wounds that were so profound to the previous individuals that they affected the consciousness as it went on to the next life, so the scars were carried over into the next body.

A disadvantage of this explanation is that the term reincarnation does not tell us everything that we would like to know. Where does the consciousness go between lives? When does it enter the new body? Why do these children have memories of past lives when most people do not? The cases offer some hints to these questions, as we will see in the upcoming chapters, but no definitive answers are available. And then the biggest question of them all is this: If these children had previous lives, does that mean that we all reincarnate? We can only speculate about this one, and we will do so later in the book.

If we accept for the moment the possibility that Abby's case is an example of reincarnation, then we need to think about what we can learn from it. Abby, like most of these children, did not talk about any experiences between lives, so she did not say how and why she came back. To consider why she might have been reborn to Abby's mother in particular, we should recognize that her mother and great-grandmother had a close connection. Since they had some conflict during her mother's teen years, the great-grandmother may have returned to work out their differences. Her mother said that they had already reconciled while the great-grandmother was still alive, so what seems more likely is that she would have been drawn to Abby's mother because of the positive aspects of their relationship.

Abby's case sheds almost no light on how that occurred, if it did. We do not know if her great-grandmother chose to be born to Abby's mother or chose to be born at all. Perhaps she did not make a conscious decision to return but was drawn to Abby's mother in an emotional way analogous to a magnetic attraction. We can only speculate. We will examine cases in which the children have described memories of events between lives, and we can see if those cases provide any clues as to what happens to lead an individual to return to one particular set of parents. For now, we must be content with the awareness that cases like Abby's suggest that the relationships that we have in one lifetime may be capable of continuing to the next.

Let us look back at Abby's case now with the entire list of explanations in mind. The most likely *normal* explanation is probably that of faulty memory by the informant, in this case the mother.

The other explanations do not seem as reasonable. Though Abby's mother could have made up the story, there is no evidence of fraud and no apparent motivation for it. Abby seems unlikely to have come up with her great-grandmother's name simply by coincidence. Even if Abby knew her great-grandmother's name because she had heard it, this would not explain why she thought that she had been her great-grandmother and why she could not tell her mother the name a few days later. That leaves Abby's mother recalling their conversation incorrectly as the best explanation that uses normal processes, despite the fact that she was fully aware of the significance of Abby's answer before Abby gave it, meaning that she focused on it, improving her chances of recalling it correctly.

Part of the attraction of this explanation is the feeling, "That couldn't have happened; her mother must be mistaken." In other words, if her mother has remembered that conversation correctly, then we have trouble explaining the case by normal means. This means that we need to consider paranormal means. Among those possibilities, reincarnation is more plausible for this case than either ESP or possession.

The choice seems to boil down to reincarnation or a case in which Abby's mother embellished the story, either intentionally in the case of fraud or accidentally in the case of faulty memory. Which one do we think is the best explanation? The answer at this point must be that we do not yet have enough information. Critics would surely say that one curious conversation does not prove anything, and it is certainly not enough to alter our view of the world radically. We should remember though that this topic involves more than just one conversation. Along with Abby's case, dozens of other American cases exist, many of which involve parents who had never given reincarnation a second thought before their children started talking. We must also consider the hundreds of cases of children from other cultures, some with birthmarks matching wounds on the deceased, some with detailed knowledge about strangers from distant places, and some with desperate longings to return to the previous family or dramatic behaviors matching the previous life. Abby's case is not even one of the stronger ones.

Let us not dismiss the whole matter until we have reviewed it fully. Perhaps we are being premature at this point even to ask what explains this phenomenon, but this question lurks behind every aspect of the cases that we will explore. We will therefore return to it as we look at each type of case.

CHAPTER 4

Marked for Life

Patrick Christenson is a boy who was born by cesarean section in Michigan in 1991. When the nurses brought him to his mother, she immediately felt that he was connected to her first son, who had died of cancer at the age of two in 1979, twelve years earlier. She soon noticed that Patrick displayed three defects that matched those her other son had when he died.

Her first son, Kevin, began to limp when he was one and a half years old. One day, he fell and broke his left leg. This led to a medical workup that included a biopsy of a nodule on his scalp above his right ear. Doctors diagnosed him with metastatic cancer. A bone scan showed many abnormal sites. His left eye was protruding and bruised due to a tumor. He received chemotherapy through a central line, a large IV line, in the right side of his neck. Though the site on his neck where the chemotherapy agents were entering his body became flushed and slightly swollen several times, he had no major problems with the treatment and was eventually discharged home. He received outpatient treatment but returned to the hospital five months later. At that point, he appeared blind in his left eye. He was admitted with a fever, treated with antibiotics, and discharged from the hospital. He died two days later, three weeks after his second birthday.

Kevin's parents had separated before his death, and his mother eventually remarried. She gave birth to a daughter and son before Patrick was born. At birth, he had a slanting birthmark with the appearance of a small cut on the right side of his neck—the same location of Kevin's central line—a nodule on his scalp above his right ear as Kevin's biopsied tumor had been, and an opacity in his left eye, diagnosed as a corneal leukoma, that caused him, like Kevin, to have very little vision in that eye. When he began walking, he limped, favoring his left leg.

When Patrick was almost four and a half years old, he began telling his mother things that she felt were related to the life of Kevin. He talked for some time about wanting to go back to their previous home and told his mother that he had left her there. He said that the home was orange and brown, which was correct. He asked his mother if she remembered him having surgery, and when she replied that he had not had any surgery, he said that he had and pointed to the area above his right ear where Kevin had his nodule biopsied. He also said that he did not remember the actual surgery because he was asleep when it was done. At another time, Patrick saw a picture of Kevin, whose pictures were not normally displayed in the family's home, and said that the picture was of him.

After Patrick began making these statements, his mother contacted Carol Bowman, an author who has written two books about children who talk about previous lives—*Children's Past Lives* and *Return from Heaven*. They talked on the phone a number of times, with Carol offering guidance on how to deal with the past-life issues that seemed to be coming up. She eventually referred the case to us for investigation. Dr. Stevenson and I then visited the family when Patrick was five years old.

While we were there, we saw and photographed the birthmark on Patrick's neck, a 4-millimeter dark slanting line on the lower part of the right side of his neck that looked like a healed cut. The nodule on his head was very hard to see but easy to palpate, so we documented the small mass we felt there. We could see the opacity in Patrick's left eye and obtained copies of the eye exams he had received. We watched him walk and could easily determine that he had a slight limp, despite having no medical condition that would explain it. We obtained Kevin's medical records, and they documented the history described earlier, including the lesions that appeared to correspond to Patrick's subsequent birthmarks. We took Patrick to the home that Kevin had shared with his mother. Patrick, unfortunately, did not have great enunciation and could be difficult to understand at times, but he did not make any statements that definitely indicated that he recognized the home.

In summary, Patrick had three unusual lesions at birth that appeared to correspond to lesions that his half-brother Kevin had suffered. In addition, he limped when he began walking and also alluded to events in Kevin's life when talking to his mother.

Patrick's case is an example of the birthmark and birth defect cases that Dr. Stevenson wrote about in *Reincarnation and Biology: A Contribution to the Etiology of Birthmarks and Birth Defects,* in which he presents numerous cases of children who have not only reported past-life memories but also have birthmarks or birth defects that appear to match wounds on the body of the previous personality. They come from various parts of thc world, and they have many different types of birthmarks and birth defects. Though

I will not attempt to summarize all 225 cases in the book, some cases are especially worth highlighting.

The Case of Chanai Choomalaiwong

Chanai Choomalaiwong was born in central Thailand in 1967 with two birthmarks, one on the back of his head and one above his left eye. When he was born, his family did not think that his birthmarks were particularly significant, but when he was three years old, he began talking about a previous life. He said that he had been a schoolteacher named Bua Kai and that he had been shot and killed while on the way to school. He gave the names of his parents, his wife, and two of his children from that life, and he persistently begged his grandmother, with whom he lived, to take him to his previous parents' home in a place called Khao Phra.

Eventually, when he was still three years old, his grandmother did just that. She and Chanai took a bus to a town near Khao Phra, which was fifteen miles from their home village. After the two of them got off the bus, Chanai led the way to a house where he said his parents lived. The house belonged to an elderly couple whose son, Bua Kai Lawnak, had been a teacher who was murdered five years before Chanai was born. Chanai's grandmother, it turned out, had previously lived three miles away. Since she had a stall where she sold goods to many people in the surrounding area, she vaguely knew Bua Kai and his wife. She had never been to their home and had no idea to whose home Chanai was leading her. Once there, Chanai identified Bua Kai's parents, who were there with a number of other family members, as his own. They were impressed enough by his statements and his birthmarks to invite him to return a short time later. When he did, they tested him by asking him to pick out Bua Kai's belongings from others, and he was able to do that. He recognized one of Bua Kai's daughters and asked for the other one by name. Bua Kai's family accepted that Chanai was Bua Kai reborn, and he visited them a number of times. He insisted that Bua Kai's daughters call him "Father," and if they did not, he refused to talk to them.

As for Bua Kai's wounds, no autopsy report was available, but Dr. Stevenson talked with a number of family members about his injuries, and they said that he had two wounds on his head from being shot. His wife remembered that the doctor who examined Bua Kai's body said that the entrance wound was the one on the back of his head because it was much smaller than the wound on his forehead that would have been the exit wound. These matched Chanai's birthmarks: a small, circular one on the back of his head and a larger, more irregular one on the front. They were both hairless and puckered. No one photographed them until Chanai was eleven and a half years old, so determining exactly where they were on his head at birth is difficult. In the photographs, the larger one is on the left toward the top of his head in front, but witnesses said that it had been lower on his forehead when he was younger.

In this case, a number of witnesses stated that a young child with birthmarks that matched the entrance and exit wounds on a deceased man had knowledge about that man's life that he seemingly could not have obtained through normal means, and he was able to pass tests that the man's family constructed for him.

The Case of Necip Ünlütaşkiran

Another case from *Reincarnation and Biology* is that of Necip Ünlütaşkiran from Turkey. At the time of his birth, he was noted to have a number of birthmarks on his head, face, and trunk. His parents initially named him Malik, but three days after his birth, his mother had a dream in which her baby told her that he was called Necip. The parents then chose to change his name to Necati instead of Necip, since the names were similar and another child in the family was already named Necip. When the boy became old enough to speak, he insisted that his name was really Necip and refused to answer to anything else, so his parents eventually agreed to call him Necip.

Necip was slow in speaking and late in speaking about a previous life, but when he was six years old, he began saying that he had children. He gradually gave other details, including the fact that he had been stabbed repeatedly. He said he had lived in the city of Mersin, fifty miles from the family's home. The family did not immediately take him there, because of their lack of means as well as their lack of interest in what he was saying.

When Necip was twelve years old, his mother took him to a town near Mersin to visit her father and his wife, whom neither Necip nor his mother had met before. When Necip did meet her, he said that she was now his real grandmother after being only like a grandmother to him in the past. He told her about his memories of a previous life, and she confirmed that they were true. She had previously lived in Mersin, where she was known as "Grandmother." A neighbor of hers there named Necip Budak had been stabbed and killed shortly before the child Necip was born. Necip's grandfather then took him to Mersin, where he recognized a number of Necip Budak's family members. He identified two items that had belonged to Necip Budak, and he correctly said that Necip Budak had once cut his wife on her leg with a knife during an argument. The boy had not seen the widow's legs, of course, but a woman in Dr. Stevenson's group examined them and confirmed that she had a scar on her thigh that she said her husband had given her.

Dr. Stevenson was able to obtain a copy of Necip Budak's autopsy report, and he found that Necip the boy had three birthmarks, ones that his family had noted at his birth that were still visible when Dr. Stevenson examined him at age thirteen, that matched wounds described in the autopsy report. In addition, Necip had previously had three birthmarks that his family noted at birth that were no longer visible at age thirteen that matched wounds in the report. Dr. Stevenson also found two marks on Necip that corresponded to wounds in the report, but his parents had not noticed these marks before. Lastly, the autopsy described a number of wounds on the left arm of Necip Budak that did not match any birthmarks on Necip the boy.

In summary, Necip had up to eight birthmarks that matched documented wounds on Necip Budak, who was killed fifty miles away, and he also gave correct details about Necip Budak's life and recognized his family members.

In the two cases I have just described, the subject had a very slight connection to the previous personality. Chanai's grandmother had known the previous personality somewhat, and Necip's step-grandmother had known his previous personality well. In most of the cases in *Reincarnation and Biology,* the connection is even stronger than these are. Many of them are either same-family cases or ones in which the child and the previous personality lived in the same village or at least in villages close to each other.

We can look at these connections in different ways. One explanation in many of the cases is that the child's birthmark pointed to a likely previous personality since someone had died in the area with a similar wound. Relatively few statements were then required from the child to confirm the match. For example, in one case, a man died from a shotgun blast to the lower chest, and a child was later born in the same village with a birthmark that looked exactly like a shotgun blast on his lower chest. Consequently, his family suspected that he was the deceased man returned. He then only had to make a few statements about the previous life—including that he was the previous personality and that he had been shot in the chest—before he was accepted as the reincarnation of the deceased man.

On the other hand, if a child is born with a similar birthmark, but no one nearby has died from such an injury, then he must give more details in order for the case to be solved. In particular, he must give the location of the previous personality, and he must get his parents interested enough in the case to go to the other location to try to solve it. Obviously, a nearby birthmark case develops much more easily than a long-distance one.

The cases of Chanai and Necip, despite their slight connections to the previous personalities, do not particularly fit this pattern, because their birthmarks did not lead their parents to think of one particular previous personality. In Chanai's case, his grandmother did not associate him with the previous personality until Chanai took her to the home of that man's parents. In Necip's case, the previous personality would not have been identified except for the fact that the boy recognized his grandfather's wife as someone he had known from his previous life.

A skeptical reader might conclude that the connections in these cases led people to identify the children as rebirth cases erroneously. The idea would be that the families must have known enough about the previous personalities either to share the information with the boys or to infer that the boys were talking about particular deceased individuals when they were not. The next two cases are not open to that criticism, since no connection existed between the two families at all.

The Case of Indika Ishwara

Indika Ishwara, an identical twin, was born in Sri Lanka in 1972. His brother talked about a previous life at an early age, as I will discuss in Chapter 6. When Indika was three years old, he also began talking about one. He said that he was from Balapitiya, a town nearly thirty miles from his hometown. He talked about his previous parents. He did not give their names but referred to them as his Ambalangoda mother and Ambalangoda father. He said that he attended a big school in Ambalangoda, a larger town near to Balapitiya, and that he traveled there by train. He said that he was called "Baby Mahattaya." *Mahattaya* means "master" or "boss" in Sinhalese, and Baby Mahattaya is a fairly common nickname in Sri Lanka. He claimed he had an older sister named Malkanthie, with whom he had bicycled. He described an uncle named Premasiri as well as a "Mudalali Bappa." *Mudalali* means an individual with a substantial business, and *bappa* means a paternal uncle. He mentioned that the family had a calf and a dog and said that a car and a truck were at the home.

In addition, he talked of going with his sister to the temple, where he said a red curtain hung in front of the Buddha image. He said that his previous father wore trousers; his own father wore a sarong. His previous home, where a wedding had taken place, had electricity. His family's home did not. He described his previous mother as being darker, taller, and fatter than his present one. He said that he had gone to school through the fourth grade and had a classmate named Sepali.

Indika's family did not know anyone who lived in Ambalangoda. His father had a friend who worked there, and he asked the friend to try to locate the previous personality's family based on what Indika had said. The friend quickly located a family in Balapitiya who seemed to fit Indika's statements. Their oldest son, Dharshana, had died at ten of viral encephalitis four years before Indika was born.

The friend spoke with Dharshana's mother about Indika, since Dharshana's father was away at the time. When the father learned what Indika had been saying, he was quite interested, and he soon made an unannounced trip to Indika's hometown. He went to the shop of Indika's father. While he was waiting there for someone to take him to the family's home, an employee asked him if he had a daughter named Malkanthie and a son called Mahatmaya, since Indika had been reporting these things. He did, and he then went to the family's home and met Indika, who was not yet four years old. People thought that Indika recognized him, because even though he did not call him by name directly, he said to his mother, "Father has come."

Shortly after that, various members of Dharshana's family

made two trips to see Indika. Indika was thought to recognize several of them, but their interactions occurred in uncontrolled conditions with a lot of people around. Dr. Stevenson's longtime associate in Sri Lanka, Godwin Samararatne, later accompanied Indika to Balapitiya and Ambalangoda, but Indika did not say anything that suggested that he recognized anything he saw. At that point, most of Dharshana's family members had already met Indika, but Mr. Samararatne was able to set up controlled tests to see if Indika could recognize an additional uncle and cousin. He did not. On his second visit to Dharshana's family, he appeared to be looking for something outside a house in the family's compound. He discovered what he had been looking for and pointed out Dharshana's name and the date 1965 that had been scratched, presumably by Dharshana, in the wall of a concrete drain when the concrete was still wet. No one in Dharshana's family knew about this or had ever noticed the writing until Indika pointed it out to them.

Mr. Samararatne, Dr. Stevenson's associate, had learned of the case soon after it developed, and he conducted interviews with Indika's parents three weeks after the initial meeting between Indika and Dharshana's father, and with Dharshana's father a week after that. All of Indika's statements about the previous life in these pages come from those initial interviews that occurred very soon after the families first met. The memory that Dharshana's father had of hearing the two names at the shop of Indika's father seems particularly striking, and I think we must conclude that Indika gave those names before the families ever met.

Almost all of the statements that Indika made proved to be correct for the life of Dharshana. Dharshana's family did live in Balapitiya, and he attended school in Ambalangoda. Dharshana was called "Baby Mahattaya" as a nickname. His older sister was named Malkanthie, and they did bicycle together. One of his uncles was named Premasiri (his full name was Sangama Premasiri de Silva), and a paternal uncle was a contractor and a timber merchant, thus a *mudalali*. Dharshana's family had a car and a dog. Though they did not own a truck, one was parked in the family's compound. Likewise, the family did not own a calf, but other people brought their calves to graze on the grass at the family's compound.

The temple that Indika's family attended had a white curtain in front of its image of Buddha, while the one that Dharshana's family attended had a red one. Dharshana's father did wear trousers, and the family's home did have electricity. Though Dharshana may not have witnessed a wedding directly in the family's home, several had taken place nearby, including one in a neighbor's house a few weeks before Dharshana died. Dharshana had fallen from a wall during the wedding, and his doctors later thought he might have sustained a head injury then that was related to his subsequent encephalitis. Indika's description of Dharshana's mother was accurate. Dharshana attended school through grade 4. He was just starting grade 5 when he became ill. As far as Dharshana's family and one of his classmates could recall, he did not have a classmate named Sepali.

How Indika could possibly have known all these details about an ordinary boy who died in another village almost thirty miles away is certainly worth wondering about. In addition, he had a nasal polyp his parents noticed when he was a year old. Though nasal polyps are not unusual in later ages, they are quite rare in infancy, and Indika's identical twin did not have one. So why did Indika have one? If we accept the possibility that some birthmarks and defects may arise through the process of reincarnation, one possibility to consider is that since Dharshana, the previous personality, had received both nasal oxygen and a nasal feeding tube during his illness, an irritation from one of those could have produced the subsequent polyp in Indika. The nasal polyp, though not as dramatic as some of the unusual deformities in *Reincarnation and Biology,* is rare and has no known cause, and the explanation that it somehow mirrored irritation from the nasal tubes that Dharshana had is consistent with the numerous statements that Indika made that were correct for Dharshana's life.

The Case of Purnima Ekanayake

The last case of this type that I want to present does not come from *Reincarnation and Biology*. Instead, our colleague Erlendur Haraldsson investigated and published this case. Purnima Ekanayake, a girl in Sri Lanka, was born with a group of light-colored birthmarks over the left side of her chest and her lower ribs. She began talking about a previous life when she was between two and a half and three years old, but her parents did not initially pay much attention to her statements. When she was four years old, she saw a television program about the Kelaniya temple, a well-known temple that was 145 miles away, and said that she recognized it. Later, her father, a school principal, and her mother, a teacher, took a group of students to the Kelaniya temple. Purnima went with the group on the visit. While there, she said that she had lived on the other side of the river that flowed beside the temple grounds.

By the time she was six, Purnima had made some twenty statements about the previous life, describing a male incense maker who was killed in a traffic accident. She had mentioned the names of two incense brands, Ambiga and Geta Pichcha. Her parents had never heard of these, and when Dr. Haraldsson later checked the shops in their town, none of them sold those brands of incense.

A new teacher began working in Purnima's town. He spent his weekends in Kelaniya where his wife lived. Purnima's father told him what Purnima had said, and the teacher decided to check in Kelaniya to see if anyone had died there who matched her statements. The teacher said that Purnima's father gave him the following items to check:

- She had lived on the other side of the river from the Kelaniya temple.
- She had made Ambiga and Geta Pichcha incense sticks.
- She was selling incense sticks on a bicycle.
- She was killed in an accident with a big vehicle.

He then went with his brother-in-law, who did not believe in reincarnation, to see if a person matching those statements could be located. They went to the Kelaniya temple and took a ferry across the river. There, they asked about incense makers and found that three small family incense businesses were in the area. The owner of one of them called his brands Ambiga and Geta Pichcha. His brother-in-law and associate, Jinadasa Perera, had been killed by a bus when he was taking incense sticks to the market on his bicycle two years before Purnima was born.

Purnima's family visited the owner's home soon after. There, Purnima made various comments about family members and their business that were correct, and the family accepted her as being Jinadasa reborn. Dr. Haraldsson began investigating the case when Purnima was nine years old. He recorded the twenty statements that her parents said Purnima had made before the two families met. In addition to the ones already mentioned, they included the names of Jinadasa's mother and wife and the name of the school that Jinadasa had attended. Dr. Haraldsson verified that fourteen of the statements were accurate for the life of Jinadasa. Three were incorrect, and the accuracy of three of them could not be determined. He also obtained Jinadasa's autopsy report, which documented fractured ribs on the left, a ruptured spleen, and abrasions running diagonally from the right shoulder across the chest to the left lower abdomen. These corresponded to the birthmarks that Purnima had over her chest and ribs.

This case challenges attempts to write off this work with a quick, normal explanation. The two families, living 145 miles apart, were, by all accounts, complete strangers to each other, and Purnima had no way of learning about Jinadasa's death before they met. Coincidence seems very unlikely, given the specificity of Purnima's statements, including the names of the incense brands. The various informants could all have faulty memories perhaps, but this case is strengthened by the presence of the intermediary, the teacher, who was independent of the two families and searched for the previous personality before they met. The birthmark is also large and prominent, and it fits nicely with the injuries of the previous personality.

A Way to Understand the Birthmark Cases

We may well wonder, even if we believe in reincarnation, how an injury to one body could then show up on the next one. We can understand how this might be possible by looking at research that has examined the interaction between psychological and physical issues. To start with, studies have shown that mental factors can produce general changes in the body. For instance, stress can contribute to illness, because it produces changes in hormones and nerve pathways that cause the immune system to be less able to fight off infections. Likewise, hopelessness has been shown to increase the risk of a heart attack or cancer. What is far less accepted, and understood not at all, is the idea that individual mental images can produce very specific changes in the body, and this is what we need to consider in order to make sense of the birthmark cases.

Dr. Stevenson presents evidence at the start of *Reincarnation and Biology*. He begins with stigmata. These are skin wounds that some usually very devout individuals develop that match the crucifixion wounds of Jesus as described in the Bible. St. Francis of Assisi may well have been the first stigmatic, and since his time, more than 350 others have been reported. These cases were first thought to represent miracles, but they were observed to occur in individuals who could not be described as saintly. They have often occurred when the individual has engaged in a particularly intense religious practice, and they have come to be regarded as psychosomatic in origin. While some cases of fraud have been exposed—individuals who intentionally created the wounds by using chemical irritants or even paint—many cases have been documented in which we can reasonably eliminate artificially induced wounds as a possibility. Thus, the mental image of Jesus' wounds in the mind of a particularly susceptible person can produce very specific changes on the skin that match the mental images.

Another example of changes in the body that the mind can produce occurs with certain individuals under hypnosis. As Dr. Stevenson notes, suggestion under hypnosis has been shown capable of producing various changes in the body; for example, not just the sensation of thirst but also changes in the kidneys that occur during dehydration, changes in heart rate, control of bleeding, changes in the timing of a woman's menstrual cycle, even enlargement of the breasts.

In addition to these, a number of cases have been published in which hypnotists produced blisters on subjects by saying that they were being burned and then touching the subjects with a cool object, such as the tip of a finger. In some cases, the hypnotists used an object in the shape of a letter or other recognizable symbol, and the subsequent wounds that were produced were in that shape. One case involved both stigmata and hypnosis, as a subject was induced under hypnosis to produce bleeding wounds on her feet and palms along with a number of triangular wounds on her forehead that looked as if a crown of thorns might have made them.

In another type of case, subjects have "relived" traumatic experiences with the help of either hypnosis or drugs and then developed skin manifestations that matched those they experienced during the original experiences. In onc notable case, a man reexperienced an event that included having his arms tied behind his back with rope. He developed deep indentations on his forearms that looked like rope marks. Mainstream science has had difficulty determining a mechanism that would explain such cases, so it has largely ignored them.

We can all agree that hypnosis can use mental images to produce at least some physiological changes in certain individuals. For instance, if a person is reliving a frightening event under hypnosis, she may develop an increased heart rate. In fact, many individuals may develop an increased heart rate by simply recalling a frightening event, even without undergoing hypnosis. In that case, we can, without too much trouble, map out the mechanism similar to the "fight or flight" response that a person develops when faced with an actual experience that is frightening or dangerous. We cannot yet map out the mechanism to explain how a person can develop blisters while thinking that he is being burned or rope marks while reliving an incident of being tied up, but we can see that such cases vary only by degree from ones in which physiological changes that we can readily explain are produced by similar mental image stimuli.

The point of all this is that the mind can produce changes in the body that, given our current state of knowledge, we are unable to explain. When I say the mind, I do not necessarily mean the brain. I am referring to the world of thoughts, or the consciousness, that exists in the brain, and I will discuss this more when I address materialism in Chapter 9. If this consciousness or mind can exist after the brain dies—if some part of us survives when our bodies die—and can enter a fetus to be reborn, then it follows that it can produce changes in the development of that fetus, just as it can produce changes during a life. Since we may assume that the period of development in the womb would be a particularly vulnerable time for the body to be affected, we can easily see that if a mind occupied a fetus while carrying traumatic memories, which previous studies have shown can produce specific lesions on the skin of certain individuals, those memories could produce birthmarks or even birth defects that matched wounds that the mind had experienced in its previous life. If the mind does survive one life and moves on to another, the birthmark cases could logically involve the same process as the previously documented hypnosis cases.

Our birthmark cases often seem to fit this model. In Patrick's case, he had marks and defects that seemed to correspond to lesions that his half-brother Kevin had experienced. Accepting for a moment that Patrick is the rebirth of Kevin, his having those lesions might seem unfair after he already had to suffer through the original traumas as Kevin, but the natural process of the mind affecting the body could produce those defects, even if we wish that such were not the case. Patrick's birthmarks are different from many of the birthmark cases in that his birthmarks do not match fatal wounds on his half-brother Kevin, who of course did not die violently, but instead match scars or deficits that would have been particularly troubling to Kevin—the scalp scar where a tumor was biopsied, the neck scar where the toddler had a central line inserted, the opacity in the left eye where he could not see, and eventually the limp matching Kevin's difficulty in walking. All of these must have been hard for young Kevin to handle, and such traumatic memories may have produced scars on Patrick's developing fetus even though they were not fatal wounds.

The same logic could apply in Indika's case of the nasal polyp corresponding to the nasal tubes that his previous personality experienced at the end of his life. In the case of Chanai, being shot and killed would clearly be a traumatic experience to a surviving mind, and similarly, Purnima's birthmarks correspond to the physically and emotionally traumatic injuries that her previous personality suffered when he was hit by a bus.

Necip's case is a little more complicated. If we accept for a moment that he might have been the reincarnation of Necip Budak, then we may wonder why he had birthmarks that matched some of Necip Budak's wounds but not others. Dr. Stevenson has suggested that in an attack, earlier wounds would be more likely to carry over to the next life because the victim would be more fully conscious when he or she received them. In this case, Necip's most prominent birthmarks were on his head, and he also had birthmarks on his chest and abdomen. Necip Budak had head wounds, but the chest and abdomen ones were the fatal ones. Dr. Stevenson suggests that if Necip Budak received his head wounds before the fatal chest and abdomen wounds, then they would have been in his mind longer before he lost consciousness.

The difficulty comes, as Dr. Stevenson likes to point out, because the people who perform autopsies do not work for us, and they often make no attempt to determine the order of wounds. In this case, Necip Budak may have been groggy after being hit on the head, so the other wounds had less impact on his mind and subsequently on his new body. We have no way of knowing. One likely scenario is that the cuts on his left arm came when he was trying to defend himself, so he would have had at least some conscious awareness. Nonetheless, Necip the boy, as noted above, did not have any birthmarks on his arm.

Another possibility to consider is that the wounds that are the most traumatic emotionally have the greatest likelihood of carrying over to the next life. These would often be the ones received when the person was first attacked and fully conscious, but this might not always be the case. Necip Budak was presumably as conscious when he received the cuts on his arm as when he received the ones on his body, but Necip the boy had no birthmarks on his arm. We can conjecture that after Necip Budak received blows to his head when he was fully conscious, the cuts he received on his body were more emotionally traumatic to him than the cuts on his arm, because they were more life-threatening. Therefore, the most prominent birthmarks occurred on Necip's head, and he also had less prominent marks on his body.

Still another possibility, of course, is that the wounds on his body led to birthmarks because the body wounds were more serious injuries than the cuts on his arm. Dr. Stevenson has noted though that the fatal wound does not always produce the most significant birthmark, so a factor other than just the severity of a wound must be involved. Presumably, it involves some factor related to consciousness, perhaps either the level of consciousness at the time of the injury or the emotional impact on the individual's consciousness.

Questions About Birthmark Cases

In surveying the cases, a question that arises is if trauma at the end of a life can produce birthmarks and birth defects in the next one, why are more babies not born with marks or defects? An explanation for this involves an idea I alluded to earlier. In the discussion on hypnosis, I said that it could produce changes in certain individuals. Some people respond to hypnosis much more strongly than others. In fact, some cannot be hypnotized at all. In the case of rebirth, we might also expect that some individuals would be more susceptible than others to having lesions on the new body produced by past-life trauma. Hypnosis is unable to produce marks on the skin of most people, but some subjects are particularly susceptible to it. Likewise, injuries at death may be unlikely to affect the next life's fetus for most individuals, but some may be particularly susceptible to it.

We do not have any clear sense of what factors might determine how susceptible a particular individual would be to trauma transfer, but one may be cultural beliefs. If a general belief in the culture supports the possibility that past-life trauma can affect a developing fetus, then individuals in that culture might be more susceptible to developing lesions than individuals in other cultures. In hypnosis, the subject's expectations for what can happen under hypnosis can have an effect on what does happen. Likewise, an individual's beliefs about life and death may affect such subsequent occurrences as birthmarks. This could explain, at least in part, why the birthmarks occur more frequently in some places than in others. Patrick's case notwithstanding, we have very few birthmark cases from the United States. The lack of acceptance of the phenomenon here may cause Americans to be less prone to developing past-life trauma birthmarks than people in other places.

Having said that, I should point out that the birthmark cases do not necessarily correspond to the religious beliefs held in many of the communities where the cases are found. The concept of *karma,* which is so central to Hindu and Buddhist beliefs, holds that the conditions into which a person is born are determined by his or her conduct in previous lives. Based on that, we might think that following a murder, the killer and not the victim would bear the birthmarks or birth defects in the next life as a result of karmic debt, but that is not what we see. We have only three cases in which the children thought that their birth defects were retribution for acts they remembered in a prior life. One subject, a boy in Sri Lanka named Wijeratne, remembered the life of his uncle, who had been hanged eighteen years before Wijeratne's birth for stabbing a woman after she called off their marriage. Wijeratne was born with a deformed right arm and hand, both being much shorter than normal, and an absent pectoral muscle on the right side of his chest. Wijeratne said that he had a defective hand because he had killed the woman with his hand in his previous life.

In all the other cases, the children described getting wounds in the previous life that carried over to their new bodies, so the patterns in the cases seem more consistent with the idea of mental images or memories producing bodily changes. Nonetheless, individuals in these cultures seem more open generally to spiritual effects on health or on the body, so such openness may make them more susceptible to having past-life birthmarks even if the marks do not conform to their notions of karma.

Beyond the cultural differences, we also need to consider differences in individuals. Even though a past-life cause for birthmarks and birth defects is accepted much more easily in many countries than it is in ours, expectations among individuals may vary a great deal. People in the cultures where most of the cases are found have varying degrees of belief in reincarnation, just as religious beliefs in the United States vary from individual to individual, and the degree of belief and expectation in an individual mind may affect the likelihood of subsequent birthmarks. Similarly, the general cultural beliefs in the U.S. do not include a belief in reincarnation, but some individuals do expect to be reborn. An example is William, the boy I presented in Chapter 1 who was born with the heart defect that matched the fatal wounds that his grandfather received in a shooting. His grandfather was a practicing Roman Catholic, but he also had a belief in reincarnation. That belief conceivably could have made him more susceptible to having a birth defect related to his fatal wounds in his next life.

Another question that comes up is why so many of the cases involve the skin. Some involve such deformities as missing digits or limbs, but only a few involve internal diseases. We can only speculate about the reasons for this, but it may also relate to being a phenomenon of consciousness. We are much more conscious of lesions of the skin than we are of lesions of internal organs, so we might then be more likely to carry the memory of those lesions to the next life. Likewise, if a man has his fingers cut off while being killed, he is surely aware of that happening, but he may not be aware, for instance, of his liver being lacerated by a bullet. Deformities may arise due to the previous personality's awareness of the injuries, and internal organs may be spared because the victim is not aware of the specific injuries.

William's case is an exception to this. If his heart defect is a manifestation of his grandfather's injuries, we may wonder why he did not at least have a birthmark on his chest to go along with the heart defect. I do not have a definitive answer to that question, but I wonder if the grandfather thought that the chest pain he was feeling meant that he had been hit in the heart. He would have focused more on his heart than on his skin. To complicate matters, even though William did not have a birthmark on his chest to coincide with his heart defect, he did have a birthmark on his neck that may relate to his grandfather's death. Carol Bowman referred me to William and his mother. When I first met with them, his mother did not report that he had any birthmarks. In our subsequent correspondence, she noted that he did have one on his neck below his left ear, and she sent me a picture of it. This birthmark is in the same location as an area of bruising on the neck of William's grandfather that his autopsy documented. That bruise must have been severe, because it was included in the autopsy's one-paragraph description of the external examination of the body. William's mother, in fact, thought that her father had been shot there, but since the autopsy does not indicate an entrance or exit wound there, the bruising likely came from a bullet grazing that area of his neck. Along with a heart defect that matches trauma that his grandfather suffered, William has a birthmark corresponding to a bruise but not any birthmarks that match the various entrance and exit wounds that bullets created on his grandfather's body. To speculate on this, perhaps William's grandfather was conscious of the injury to his neck before focusing on the fatal heart trauma, and he did not focus particularly on the impact of the other bullets.

William's case also indicates a practical factor that may be involved in producing few cases of internal organ defects. A baby born in an Asian village with the heart defect that William had would surely have died within a few days after birth, if not sooner. He would never have had the opportunity to talk about the previous life, and we would never have learned about the case. Perhaps cases with internal organ defects occur, but they do not become known as rebirth cases, because the children die at such an early age.

Experimental Birthmarks

As I described earlier, experimental birthmarks are practiced in several Asian countries. Someone, usually a family member or close family friend, makes a mark on the body of a dying or deceased person, often with soot or paste, in the belief that when the individual is reborn, the baby will bear a birthmark that corresponds to the mark made on the body. The marker often says a prayer while making the mark, asking that the dying person take the mark with him or her to the new body. A child is later born with a birthmark that is said to match the marking made on the body.

Dr. Stevenson was the first person in the West to fully document this practice, but other authors have mentioned it. For instance, the Dalai Lama wrote in his autobiography about a case that occurred in his family. His younger brother died at two years of age. A small mark was made on the boy's body with a smear of butter after he died, and his mother subsequently gave birth to another son who had a pale mark on his body in the same place where the first body had been marked.

That case is fairly typical of the cases that we have found. Dr. Stevenson describes twenty such cases in *Reincarnation and Biology,* and Jürgen Keil and I found eighteen more during trips to Thailand and Myanmar. In these cases, the mark is usually made with the expectation that the reincarnated individual carrying the mark will be born into the same family as the deceased individual, and fifteen of our eighteen cases were same-family. This would seem to lessen the chances that the marking and the birthmark matched simply out of coincidence, compared to a situation where any baby in the area could be considered the rebirth of the deceased individual.

In addition, in six of our eighteen cases, the children had also made statements that related to the previous life, and some of the other children were so young when we saw them that they may have later made statements. Some of the cases feature behaviors as well as statements that suggest a connection between the subject and the previous personality, while in others, the birthmark is the only sign of a connection.

One case that Dr. Keil and I investigated can serve as a good example. Kloy Matwiset is a boy who was born in Thailand in 1990. Eleven months before he was born, his maternal grandmother died of diabetes. Before she died, she told her daughter-in-law that she would like to be reborn as a male so that she could have a mistress as her husband did. The day after she died, her daughter-in-law used white paste to make a mark down the back of her neck so that she could recognize her mother-in-law when she was reborn.

Kloy's mother had an announcing dream when she was three months pregnant in which the grandmother said that she wanted to be reborn to her. His mother had seen the mark made on the grandmother's body. When Kloy was born, she noticed that he had a birthmark on the back of his neck in the same place where the mark had been made. We met him and saw a very noticeable vertical pale discoloration on the back of his neck that had a shape that matched a finger making a mark down his neck. The marker confirmed that this unusual birthmark was in the same place that she had marked his grandmother's body.

When Kloy was quite young, he made several statements about the previous life. He said that he was his grandmother and told his mother that he was her mother. He also said that his grandmother's rice field belonged to him. In addition, he showed a number of feminine behaviors. He said that he wanted to be a girl, and as a young child, he generally sat down to urinate. He also enjoyed wearing women's clothing and wore his mother's lipstick, earrings, and dresses many times. At school, he enjoyed playing and studying with the girls rather than the boys, and he did not engage in typical male behaviors for boys in that area such as climbing trees. Both of his parents complained about his feminine behaviors, and they said that they never talked to him about being the rebirth of his grandmother.

His feminine behaviors suggest that he has what is known as a gender identity disorder, and I will talk more about such behaviors in Chapter 6. I want to focus now on the birthmark and how it may have come about. One possibility, of course, is coincidence. That would not explain the other features of the case. In addition, for us to say that this unusual birthmark just happened to occur after the previous personality's daughter-in-law asked for exactly such a mark, we have to stretch the coincidence explanation beyond what may be reasonable.

Another possibility worth considering is that though the child is not the rebirth of the previous personality, the mother's wish or expectation somehow produced the mark. Since most of the experimental birthmark cases are same-family ones, the mother of the subject has often either seen the marking on the body or at least known about it. The question becomes whether her wishing or expecting to have the deceased family member reborn as her child could lead her to give birth to a child with the predicted birthmark. In considering this possibility, we need again to recall the hypnosis cases. If an image in the mind can produce a mark on a person's skin, then could an image in a mother's mind produce a mark on the skin of a developing fetus? This would be similar to cases of maternal impression, a concept popular at the end of the nineteenth century that was used to describe cases in which a pregnant mother who was troubled by the sight of a person with a physical deformity then gave birth to a child with the same defect. People eventually decided that the concept was absurd, because they could not imagine a mechanism that would explain it, though we now know that the placental barrier is a lot more porous than people previously thought. Dr. Stevenson lists various published cases of maternal impression in *Reincarnation and Biology,* and they include what would certainly be some remarkable coincidences, the most remarkable perhaps being the case of a pregnant woman who, after being quite troubled upon seeing her brother's wounds from the amputation of his cancerous penis, gave birth to a boy with a congenital absence of the penis, a condition fortunately so rare as to be almost unheard of.

In any event, the experimental birthmark cases differ from the hypnosis and maternal impression cases in at least one important way. Hypnosis is obviously an unusual state of mind, and similarly, most of the maternal impression mothers were strongly affected emotionally by the deformities they saw. In the experimental birthmark cases, the mother, though presumably upset about the death of a family member, often noted the marking but was not particularly moved by it emotionally. In addition, the mother usually saw the marking some time before she became pregnant, and while we can well imagine that pregnancy would be a particularly susceptible time for a traumatized consciousness to affect the development of a fetus, the idea that an image that the mother saw months or years before she became pregnant could produce a mark on her baby's body seems less logical. Perhaps we could consider that her expectation or wish that her child would be the rebirth of the previous personality might be strong enough to lead her to give birth to a baby with a birthmark matching the mark made on that person's body. Such an explanation of the birthmark would not, of course, explain the children's statements and behaviors in some of the cases.

As for the reincarnation possibility, we have the issue of when the bodies are marked. The markings are sometimes made when the individual is still dying, but the person has often died first. At times, the bodies may be marked a couple of days after the person has died or at the beginning of the cremation service. That being the case, more would have to be involved in producing the birthmark than simply the physical mark on the body, since a cremation immediately following it might be expected to produce results as much as a marking could, and a baby does not later show any effects from it.

At least two possibilities are worth considering. One is that the surviving consciousness can stay near the body for some time after death, which would be consistent with the occasional reports that we get from children describing the funerals of the previous personality as I will discuss in Chapter 8. A mark made on the body might produce an emotional impact that would cause the subsequent birthmark, just as wounds in the other cases can match later birthmarks on the subjects. Another possibility is that the prayer that the marker says may be more important than the marking itself. When that person asks the individual to carry the mark to the next life, the consciousness of the marker may connect with the consciousness of the deceased individual to produce the subsequent birthmark. We might speculate that the time around death would be a particularly susceptible time, and the prayer would act almost like a posthypnotic suggestion in causing the mark to appear on the future child.

In any event, these experimental birthmark cases can certainly be challenging, and they may give us clues about the phenomenon in general. They show that cases can occur that involve blemishes that are made following death as well as before. If these are cases of reincarnation, this would seem to indicate that a consciousness can be affected by events that occur for at least some period of time after death. They also suggest, to me at least, that the birthmark cases are due to more than just the physical wound on a body. This is logical in a way, since we would have trouble imagining how the consciousness might be able to carry a physical wound without the actual physical body. If we conceptualize that the physical wound produces a mental image, the idea that the mental image could affect the development of an embryo when the consciousness enters it is consistent with the effects of mental images in other special situations.

Considering the Explanations

In looking for an explanation for the birthmark cases in general, we see that in many of the cases, the family of the subject knows about the death of the previous personality before the child is born, because that person was a family member, friend, or at least an acquaintance. In such a situation, we cannot assume that the parents' knowledge about the death causes the birthmark or birth defect if we are restricting ourselves to normal explanations, but we can speculate that the mark or defect leads the parents to decide that the child is the rebirth of the deceased individual. We can then try to explain the child's past-life statements with either a scenario of knowledge acquired through normal means or one of faulty memory by informants, as follows. After deciding that the child is a rebirth case, the parents may plant the idea in the head of the young child, who comes to believe the past-life story. The child can then start to claim to be the previous personality and can also pick up tidbits about that person's life that he says are memories of the past life. In addition, in their enthusiasm, the parents may misinterpret statements by the child as showing more knowledge about the previous life than the child actually has. In either case, the parents' initial beliefs will come to be confirmed by the child's statements, and all involved will believe that the child is the previous personality reborn.

All of this goes against the frequent testimony of the families that the child possessed knowledge about the previous life that the parents feel he or she could not have learned about in this life, even though the family knew the previous personality. Regardless of that issue, we still have the birthmark or birth defect to explain, and we should remember that some of them are very unusual. In Patrick Christenson's case, he had three unusual ones, and he also developed a limp when he learned to walk. Such a combination would be unusual in any situation, but the fact that all of his defects matched ones on his deceased half-brother makes the situation rather extraordinary. Similarly, Chanai Choomalaiwong had a small, round birthmark on the back of his head that looked like a bullet entrance wound and a larger, irregular mark toward the front of his head that looked like an exit wound. Unusual by themselves, but when they are considered along with his statements about the life of a schoolteacher who was shot from behind, they become extraordinary. In these situations, the only normal explanation available to explain the birthmarks is that of coincidence, and given the unlikelihood of the matches occurring simply by chance, this explanation seems unsatisfactory.

And these are the easy cases to explain. When we look at the ones in which the subject's family had never heard of the previous personality, a normal explanation gets even tougher. Indika Ishwara and Purnima Ekanayake not only had birthmarks, but they made numerous statements about strangers who died a long distance away. The statements proved to be accurate for a specific deceased individual who had a lesion that corresponded to the child's birthmark.

We can again fall back on coincidence as a way to explain the birthmarks, but then we have to explain the statements as well. Coincidence can only go so far, and in a case like Purnima's, in which she made twenty statements about the previous personality that included details about an incense maker being killed on a bicycle and in which she even named the correct brands of incense, ones that were not available locally, coincidence is really not a realistic explanation. In such a case, we might try to use coincidence to explain the birthmark while using another explanation for the accuracy of the statements.

Knowledge acquired through normal means can be an explanation if the previous personality lived in the same community as the child, but it seems quite inadequate to explain the statements in a case such as Purnima's where the previous personality lived 145 miles from the subject's home. Another way to explain the statements is to blame faulty memory by the informants. In this explanation, Purnima and children like her did not really make the statements that they are credited with making. We do not have to say that their accuracy is an incredible coincidence because we do not give the children credit for the statements in the first place.

Thus, for the cases that have birthmarks and previous personalities who lived a significant distance away, we can say that the birthmarks occur by a strange coincidence and that the statements are remembered incorrectly. No other normal explanation really makes sense. We will come back to this question of faulty memory by informants after looking at the other types of cases.

As for the paranormal explanations, ESP cannot easily explain the birthmark cases since they obviously involve more than just the paranormal transfer of information. Similarly, possession cannot explain the birthmarks as long as we think of it as something that takes place after birth. Reincarnation, on the other hand, can explain them, as we have already discussed, by using the idea that the consciousness is so affected by the trauma that led to the injuries on the body of the previous personality that it affects the development of the fetus and produces a similar mark. Given the fact that the children also report memories of the previous life of a person who had matching injuries, reincarnation is certainly the most obvious paranormal explanation and perhaps the only viable one for this type of case.

To summarize our exploration of the birthmark cases, we can say that though most of the cases take place among family members or friends, some occur among complete strangers as well. If these are cases of reincarnation, the likely mechanism involves mental images imprinted on the surviving consciousness by trauma, and the experimental birthmark cases suggest that this imprinting can even occur for a short time after the death of the previous personality.

CHAPTER 5

Remembering the Past

Sujith Jayaratne, a boy from a suburb of the Sri Lankan capital, Colombo, began showing an intense fear of trucks and even the word *lorry,* a British word for truck that has become part of the Sinhalese language, when he was only eight months old. When he became old enough to talk, he said that he had lived in Gorakana, a village seven miles away, and that he had died after being hit by a truck.

He made numerous statements about that life. His great-uncle, a monk at a nearby temple, heard some of them and mentioned Sujith to a younger monk at the temple. The story interested this monk, so he talked with Sujith, who was a little more than two and a half years old at the time, about his memories, and then wrote up notes of the conversations before he attempted to verify any of the statements. His notes document that Sujith said that he was from Gorakana and lived in the section of Gorakawatte, that his father was named Jamis and had a bad right eye, that he had attended the *kabal iskole,* which means "dilapidated school," and had a teacher named Francis there, and that he gave money to a woman named Kusuma, who prepared string hoppers, a type of food, for him. He implied that he gave money to the Kale Pansala, or Forest Temple, and said two monks were there, one of whom was named Amitha. He said that his house was whitewashed, that its lavatory was beside a fence, and that he bathed in cool water.

Sujith had also told his mother and grandmother a number of other things about the previous life that no one wrote down until after the previous personality had been identified. He said his name was Sammy, and he sometimes called himself "Gorakana Sammy." Kusuma, the woman he had mentioned to the monk, was his younger sister's daughter, and she lived in Gorakana and had long, thick hair. He said that his wife's name was Maggie and their daughter's was Nandanie. He had worked for the railways and had once climbed Adam's Peak, a high mountain in central Sri Lanka. He had transported arrack, a liquor that was illegally traded, in a boat that had once capsized, causing him to lose his entire shipment of arrack. He said that on the day he died, he and Maggie had quarreled. She left the house, and he then went out to the store. While he was crossing the road, a truck ran over him, and he died.

The young monk went to Gorakana to look for a family who had a deceased member whose life matched Sujith's statements. After some effort, he discovered that a fifty-year-old man named Sammy Fernando, or "Gorakana Sammy" as he was sometimes called, had died after being hit by a truck six months before Sujith was born. All of Sujith's statements proved to be correct for Sammy Fernando, except for his statement that he had died immediately when the truck hit him. Sammy Fernando died one to two hours after being admitted to a hospital following the accident.

Once Sammy Fernando was identified as the previous personality, Sujith was able to recognize several people from Sammy's life and to comment on changes that had been made in the Fernando property. He made many of the recognitions when no witnesses outside of the two families were present, but the monk heard him give the name of Sammy Fernando's nephew.

Dr. Stevenson interviewed witnesses a year after Sammy Fernando had first been identified as the previous personality. He interviewed thirty-five people as part of his investigation of the case, including Sujith, who was still talking about the previous life at the age of three and a half. Dr. Stevenson discovered that though Sujith's and Sammy's families had not known each other before the case developed, two people in Sujith's neighborhood had connections to Sammy Fernando. Sujith's family knew one of them, a former drinking buddy of Sammy's, slightly, and the other one, Sammy's younger sister, not at all. The family had no idea who Sujith was talking about until the monk went to Gorakana. In fact, neither Sujith's mother nor the monk had heard of Gorakana before the case developed, as it was a fairly small village some distance away from the Colombo area.

Sujith displayed other behaviors along with the phobia of trucks that were consistent with Sammy Fernando's life. He would pretend to drink arrack and then would act drunk. He also attempted to get arrack from neighbors, including one who obliged him until his grandmother intervened. In addition, he tried to smoke cigarettes. No one in his family drank arrack or smoked cigarettes, but Sammy Fernando consumed plenty of both. Sujith also asked for spicy foods Sammy Fernando frequently enjoyed, ones his family, who only ate them occasionally, would not normally have considered giving to a small child. In addition, he had a tendency as a toddler to be physically aggressive and to use obscenities, two habits that Sammy Fernando demonstrated when he was intoxicated. By the time Sujith was six years old, he had stopped talking about Sammy Fernando's life and displayed less of the unusual behavior that he had shown earlier. He still continued to ask for arrack if he saw others drinking it.

What are we to make of this? Though we might like to have a simple, normal explanation for the case, do we really think that all these people worked out an elaborate ruse to fool Dr. Stevenson? Or that the details Sujith gave just happened to match the life of Sammy Fernando? Or that Sammy's sister or former drinking buddy, who had no connection to Sujith's family, secretly told him these meaningless details about Sammy's life, leading him to think that he had been Sammy? We must also keep in mind that Sujith's case is just one of many, and we will review more of them shortly.

Features of Past-life Statements

Sujith's case has many of the typical features of these cases: a young child repeatedly claims to have memories of a previous life and gives enough details to identify a deceased individual whose life matched the child's statements. Let us look at the features of the statements in more detail.

AGE WHEN TALKING ABOUT A PREVIOUS LIFE

Sujith first communicated about the previous life when he was two and a half years old, and the average age is thirty-five months. In some cases, some of the communication is nonverbal, as the children make gestures related to the previous life before they have developed the language skills necessary to convey the information. Kumkum Verma, whose case I will describe shortly, did not know the word for blacksmith, so she said that her previous son worked with a hammer, and used gestures to show how a blacksmith hammered and how his bellows worked. The early age of communication seems logical, since we would expect memories of a past life, if they are present, to be there from the beginning. Nevertheless, exceptions do exist. When older children report past-life memories, they often have seen things that seemed to remind them of past events. Dr. James Matlock analyzed ninety-five cases and found that the older a subject was when first speaking of a previous life, the more likely that a reminder in the environment stimulated the initial memories.

Sujith's case is also typical in that he stopped talking about the previous life by the time he was six years old. Most of the children stop by the age of six or seven, and not only do they stop talking about the previous life, they often deny any memories of it when asked. We might wonder why this would be so. One possibility is that since this is the age when children generally start school, they may get more fully involved in this life and let the other memories go. More importantly, perhaps, this is the age when all children lose most of their early childhood memories. A toddler can know a family friend, but if that friend moves away, the child will often have no memory of the person by the age of six or seven. This has been called "early childhood amnesia," and though the reasons for it may be debatable, the phenomenon unquestionably occurs.

We would logically expect children with apparent past-life

memories to lose those memories at the same age; otherwise, we would wonder how children could keep memories older than the ones they had lost. The children vary, and some subjects report that they still have past-life memories even into adulthood just as some individuals report having a fair number of early childhood memories when they are adults. Nonetheless, the vast majority of subjects seem to have forgotten all about the past life after a few years. Among 300 cases across different cultures, the median age at which the subjects stopped talking about the previous life was seventy-two months (or six years), but that age varied quite a bit among different subjects. In particular, the subjects of solved cases tend to keep the memories longer than those of unsolved ones, presumably because visits between the families reinforce them.

DETAILS OF THE STATEMENTS

What Sujith said about the previous life is fairly typical of our cases. Since he described the life of someone who died as an adult, he mostly talked about people and places from the previous personality's adulthood. Subjects occasionally talk about older items, as Sujith did when he described the school that Sammy attended, but for the most part, they stick to items from near the end of the previous personality's life. This includes, of course, talk about the previous personality's death. Sujith described the events of the day that led up to the fatal accident and talked about the way in which the previous personality died, as 75 percent of the subjects do. This pattern is consistent with the idea of memory carrying over from one life to the next. Just as our memories in this life are sharper for more recent events than for older ones, these children focus on items from the end of the previous life as if the memories simply carried over from the time that the previous personality died.

That does not mean that the children report no memories from earlier in the previous life. Sujith's talk about Sammy's school and a teacher there involved issues that were presumably not a major concern of Sammy Fernando's at the end of his life, but this demonstrates how the children's recall of past-life events is similar to our memories as adults: Even though we usually recall the most important events from the past, we can also possess other fairly random memories from our childhoods.

Sujith's description of a violent death is typical of many of our cases. In cases in which the mode of death of the previous personality is known, 70 percent died by unnatural means. This includes drownings as well as violent deaths, either intentional as with murder or suicide or unintentional deaths from accidents. This figure is much higher than the actual proportion of deaths due to unnatural means in any of the areas where we find cases.

A skeptic might argue that people tend to talk about violent deaths more than natural ones, so children would be more likely to learn about them and thus claim to remember them. Sujith's case demonstrates the weaknesses in that argument. Sammy Fernando's death, which occurred when he stepped in front of a truck, was not so unusual that it would have been a likely topic for conversation three years after it happened. Moreover, Sujith described many details about Sammy Fernando that had nothing to do with his death and could hardly have been discussed at that point by anyone anywhere.

Though most of the children talk about dying, those statements are more common in cases in which the previous personalities died violently compared to ones where they died naturally. While

75 percent of the children overall describe the way that the previous personality died, only 57 percent do in the case of a natural death, suggesting that a death from an illness may not affect a consciousness in the same way that a sudden or violent death might. I will talk more about what the violent deaths might say about the process of reincarnation, if we accept it as a possibility, when we get to the final chapter.

MANNER OF SPEAKING

The manner in which the children talk about the previous life can vary. Some of the children speak about the past-life memories in a detached way, but many of them show great emotion as they recount events or talk about people from the previous life. Some cry on an almost daily basis to go back to their old family. On the other hand, an American girl named Olivia only talked about a past life once, when she was not yet three years old. During that one instance, her mother reported that she became completely distraught as she talked about needing to get back to her family. Olivia described her son being killed and a man grabbing her arm and refusing to let her go. She cried intensely about this for thirty minutes but then recovered, never to speak about those events again. Her case was unsolved and a mystery in more ways than one. Though there is no evidence of a link to a particular past life, it seems unusual that a child would become that upset in a game of make-believe or because of something she had heard on a television or radio.

Children do not express their apparent knowledge of the previous life as a list of objective facts but as specifics from the viewpoint of one deceased individual. Sujith did not give the facts of Sammy Fernando's life as simply details about a fifty-year-old man but as details about having been this man. He said "my wife" and "my house," showing that he identified himself as the deceased individual.

In doing so, some children use the past tense while others use the present. Sujith frequently talked about people from Sammy's life in the present tense. He was so young when he began talking about that life that we cannot be sure whether this was due to his confusing the past with the present or whether his language skills were simply too primitive to convey his thoughts clearly. Some children do confuse past and present, as they tell their parents, "You are not my parents. My parents live somewhere else." In such situations, the children understandably clamor to be taken to their "real parents." If they have not given enough information to identify the previous parents, their parents can sometimes mollify them by saying, "Yes, you had that life before, but now you are our child in this life." This helps the child distinguish the past from the present.

Some children become preoccupied with the previous life, but others show a tendency to speak with great emotion about the previous life one minute and then to go off and play the next. Some parents say that their children tend to speak about their past life at particular times. In Myanmar, this is often on "gloomy days," during overcast weather. American parents often say that their children usually speak about the previous life during such relaxed times as long car rides or after baths. For reasons that we do not understand, this material seems to be available only at certain times for some children, whereas other children seem able to talk about their memories at any time.

One thing that Sujith's case does not include—as most cases do not—is enlightened words of wisdom. Some of the children who claim to remember events between lives do occasionally make philosophical statements. When Kenny, a boy I mentioned in Chapter 1, was nine years old, he learned that a playmate had died, and told his mother, "I know that it's not good that Greg died, but it's not so bad either. I just wish that his mother knew that it's only Greg's body that is gone. Besides, God expects everyone to go to heaven sooner or later." Even in this case, it is unclear if he said this because of his memories or because of his Catholic religion.

In general, these children tend to focus on people and events from the end of the previous life, and their opinions about them are no different from the ones that we might assume the previous personality had. Some parents say that their children seem more mature or serious-minded than other children their age, but in many ways, the children are indistinguishable from their peers. If we thought that enlightenment came with the memories, we might have to assume that the children would stop being enlightened when they lost the memories. While some children have shown a tendency to be unusually religious or devout, the previous personalities in those cases have often been very devout, and this is not a general pattern for the children overall.

WRITTEN RECORDS

One way that Sujith's case is different from most of the others is that a written record of his statements was made before his previous personality was identified. The cases with written records make up only a small percentage, but this is hardly surprising. In the same-family cases, making a written record before the previous personality has been identified is hardly possible. Many of the others originate in areas where people tend to write down very little. These cases are usually ones in which the families are trying to satisfy themselves that a child is the rebirth of a specific previous personality, but they are not particularly interested in establishing proof for others to see. They might remember what the child said and may discuss it with others, but they usually do not write down the statements.

The number of cases in our research with written records, thirty-three at last count, seems minute compared to the number of cases overall. Collecting thirty-three cases in which written records document accurate statements that a child made about a past life is noteworthy, however, regardless of how many other cases without written records have been found, and we can review a couple more of them.

The Case of Kumkum Verma

Kumkum Verma, a girl in India, began talking about a previous life at the age of three and a half. She said that she had lived in Darbhanga, a city of 200,000 people that was twenty-five miles away from her village, and that Urdu Bazar was the name of the section of the city where she had been. Her father, an educated man who was a landowner, homeopathic physician, and author, did not know anyone in Urdu Bazar, a commercial district where artisans, craftsmen, and owners of small businesses lived.

Kumkum asked her family to call her Sunnary, which means beautiful, and made many statements about the previous life. Her aunt made notes of some of them six months before anyone tried to identify the previous personality. Dr. Stevenson, who met Kumkum's family when she was nine years old, obtained an

English translation of extracts of the notes, but he was unable to get the complete notebook, because it had been lost after being loaned to someone. The extracts listed eighteen statements that Kumkum made that all proved to be correct for the previous personality, including the name of Urdu Bazar, her son's name and the fact that he worked with a hammer, her grandson's name, the name of the town where her father lived, the location of his home near mango orchards, and the presence of a pond at her house. She had correctly stated that she had an iron safe at her house, a sword hanging near her cot, and a snake near the safe to which she fed milk.

Kumkum's father eventually talked about her statements to a friend who lived in Darbhanga. That friend had an employee from the Urdu Bazar section of the city, who was able to identify the previous personality, Sunnary or Sundari Mistry, whom Kumkum seemed to be describing. The previous personality's family belonged to a relatively low artisan class and would have been quite unlikely to have social contact with a family with the education and social status of Dr. Verma's family. In fact, they had little contact even after the case developed. The previous personality's grandson visited Kumkum's family twice. Dr. Verma went to Urdu Bazar once to meet the previous personality's family, but he never allowed Kumkum to go. Apparently he was not proud of his daughter's claim to have been a blacksmith's wife in her previous life.

One interesting note is that Kumkum said that she died during an altercation and that her stepson's wife had poisoned her. Sundari, who died quite unexpectedly five years before Kumkum was born, was preparing to be a witness for her son in his suit against her second husband, involving the son's belief that his stepfather had misappropriated his deceased father's money, when she died. No autopsy was performed, and Kumkum's statement that she was poisoned remained unverified.

Also of note is that Kumkum spoke with an accent different from that of her family. The family associated it with the lower classes of Darbhanga and reported that in addition, Kumkum used some unusual expressions that seemed related to the lower classes as well.

The Case of Jagdish Chandra

The case of Jagdish Chandra in India was quite old when Dr. Stevenson arrived on the scene. The subject was then in his late thirties. The subject's father, a prominent lawyer, had made a written record of the boy's statements and their verifications at the time that the case developed. Jagdish was born in a large city in northern India. When he was three and a half years old, he began saying that he had lived in Benares, a city approximately 300 miles away. He gave a number of details, and his father had several friends and colleagues talk with Jagdish so that they could confirm that he was making those statements. His father then sent a letter to the chairman of the municipal board in Benares. The chairman wrote back that he could tell whom Jagdish was referring to as soon as he read the letter and that he had made inquiries and found that most of the boy's statements were quite accurate.

Jagdish's father then sent a letter to a national newspaper asking for help in verifying the child's statements. In the letter, he said that Jagdish stated that his father was named Babuji Pandey and had a house in Benares with a big gate, a sitting room, and an underground room with an iron safe fixed in one of the walls. *Ji* added to the end of a name means *respected,* so Jagdish was saying that his father was called Babu. He added that Jagdish described a courtyard in which Babuji sat in the evenings and people gathered to drink bhang, an Indian drink. He said that Babuji received massages and put powder or clay on his face after washing it. He described two cars—which were very unusual in India in those days—and a horse-drawn carriage and said that Babuji had two deceased sons and a deceased wife. The father added that his son "described many private and family matters."

The day after this was published, Jagdish's father went to a magistrate to have Jagdish's statements officially recorded before they traveled to Benares, where the previous personality had lived. The recorded statements, in addition to those listed in the paper, included that his name had been Jai Gopal, and that his brother, who was bigger than he was, had been named Jai Mangal and had died of poisoning. The Ganges River was near the house, and the Dash Ashwamadh Ghat was there. (Ghats are piers where people go to bathe, and Babu Pandey was the supervisor of one.) A prostitute named Bhagwati had sung for Babu.

Jagdish was then taken to Benares, where all of the above statements were verified, with the exception that Babu Pandey had used automobiles but not actually owned them. Jagdish appeared to recognize people and places there.

As we look for ways to explain such cases as these, the fact that the child's statements were recorded before anyone attempted to verify them means that we can eliminate one possibility: that the families mistakenly credited the child later with more knowledge about the previous personality than he or she in fact had before the families met. That still leaves several possibilities. One is that the correct statements are coincidental. When we consider how specific some of the children's statements are—for example, Sujith's statement that his father Jamis had a bad right eye, Kumkum's statement that the previous personality kept a snake that she fed milk to, and Jagdish's descriptions of the habits of the previous personality's father—along with the proper names that they gave, coincidence seems extremely unlikely. Fraud is a possibility, but we do not see any motive for one, especially in Kumkum's case, because her father seemed embarrassed about her claim to have been a blacksmith's wife. Jagdish's father appeared interested in documenting an apparent case of reincarnation, but whether this wish could motivate a prominent lawyer to fake a case is certainly open to question. The other normal explanation left is that the children acquired the knowledge about the previous lives through normal means by hearing about the previous personalities. Though this may have been more likely for Sujith than for the other two, since his previous personality had lived closer, the idea that these children somehow learned these minute details about deceased strangers in other places without their parents' knowledge and then decided that they had been those strangers in a past life seems close to absurd.

When we remove the possibility that the children were credited with more information about the previous personality than they in fact had demonstrated, as we can do in cases in which a written record of the statements existed before they were verified, we are left with few palatable options that do not include a paranormal process. If we then find that numerous other cases exist that are similar to these cases in every way except that no written record was made before verification of the statements, can we reasonably discount the others as being situations in which the families mistakenly credited the children with more knowledge than they actually demonstrated?

The Case of Ratana Wongsombat

Ratana Wongsombat was born in Bangkok in 1964. Her adoptive father meditated once a week at the Wat Mahathat, a large temple with more than 300 monks on the other side of Bangkok from the family's home. Ratana began asking to go there. When she was fourteen months old, her father took her for the first time. While they were there, she seemed to show knowledge of the buildings. After they returned home, her father asked her where she had been before this life. She began talking about a previous life at that point and eventually told the following story. She had been a Chinese woman named Kim Lan and had stayed at the temple, where she lived in a green hut with a nun named Mae Chan. After eventually being driven from there, she moved to a district of Bangkok named Banglampoo. She said that she had had only one daughter, who lived in Kim Lan's old hometown, which she named, and Kim Lan had returned there at the end of her life, where she died after surgery. Ratana expressed displeasure that after she died as Kim Lan, her ashes had been scattered rather than buried.

Ratana's father was not familiar with a woman named Kim Lan, and he apparently made no immediate attempts to verify Ratana's statements. When Ratana was two years old, he again took her to the temple. When they passed a large group of nuns there, Ratana appeared to recognize one and called out "Mae Chan" to her. The nun did not respond to her, but Ratana told her father that she had lived with that nun in her previous life. Ratana's father returned to the temple a few days later and spoke with the nun. Her name was Mae Chee Chan Suthipat (*Mae Chee* is an honorific for nuns in Thailand meaning "mother nun"), but some people, including the previous personality, called her Mae Chan. She confirmed that almost all of the statements that Ratana had made, including all the ones listed in this summary, were correct for the life of Kim Lan Prayoon Supamitr, who died one and a half years before Ratana was born.

Kim Lan's daughter also confirmed Ratana's statements, including even the matter of her remains. Kim Lan had wanted her ashes to be buried under the bo tree at the temple complex, but when her daughter tried to honor her wish, the roots of the tree were so extensive that she ended up spreading the ashes rather than burying them.

The Case of Gamini Jayasena

Gamini Jayasena was born in Colombo, Sri Lanka, in 1962, and he began talking about a previous life before he was two years old. Over time, he gave details that included the following: He had another mother who was bigger than his present one. Someone named Nimal had bitten him. He had a schoolbag that was still sitting on a chair. He had a toy elephant that he bathed in a well. He had once fallen into a well. Someone named Charlie

Uncle had a car that he used to drive the subject to school, and Charlie Uncle's family also had a red motorcycle.

Since Gamini did not name a place or give a last name, the case might well have remained unsolved if his family had not taken a bus trip when he was two and a half years old. When the bus stopped briefly at a place called Nittambuwe, Gamini told the person next to him, a family friend, that this had been his home. That person relayed the information to Gamini's parents, who in turn told his mother's cousin, a well-known monk.

The monk decided to look into the matter, and he took the family back to Nittambuwe. They got out of the car at the place where Gamini had made his comment and began walking toward the four houses that were down the road. Gamini said that his mother lived there, but the monk decided not to proceed further. He apparently was unsure if this was the correct place and was concerned that he would likely be entering the home of a Christian family. Gamini's family thought he was probably remembering the life of a Christian because he knelt during prayer with his trunk erect rather than with his buttocks resting on his heels in the typical Buddhist position, and because he had once asked his mother to hang up a wooden cross he had found. The family returned to Colombo, but some Nittambuwe villagers had recognized the monk during the family's stop and told a family living at the place indicated by Gamini. This family, which was in fact a Christian family, had lost a son two years before Gamini was born. The boy, named Palitha, had died after a short illness. Just before getting sick, he had returned from school on vacation and left his schoolbag on a chair instead of putting it in the cupboard as he usually did, while announcing that he would not be going to school again.

He had a younger brother named Nimal, who had once bitten him.

Palitha's parents visited the monk. They gave the monk a picture of Palitha that Gamini subsequently appeared to recognize. Following that, Gamini's family returned to Nittambuwe to meet Palitha's parents. There, Gamini was judged to recognize a number of people and places. When he was taken to Palitha's school and the boardinghouse where Palitha stayed while attending school, he made additional recognitions and statements about Palitha's life.

All of Gamini's statements listed here proved to be correct for Palitha, except that Charles Senewiratne, Palitha's uncle, owned a car but did not drive Palitha to school. No possible connection could be found between Gamini's family in Colombo and Palitha's family in Nittambuwe, some twenty miles away.

In both of these cases, no written record of the children's statements was made before the previous personality was identified, but if we are going to decide that the families credited the children with more knowledge than they initially possessed—for instance, that they did not really give the proper names they were said to have given—then we have to explain why these cases would be different from the ones in which written records document that the children did in fact make very specific statements. They show that some children can make specific statements about past lives that are later found to be accurate for a particular deceased individual, and since the cases are so similar in all other ways, the ones with the written records have to make us question the explanation of falsely credited information for many of the other cases.

Making a Strong Case

In looking at cases without written records, some types are stronger than others. For instance, cases in which the children repeated their claims over and over again are stronger than ones in which they did not, because the parents had a better chance to recall accurately what the children had said even though they did not have the benefit of notes.

Another feature that strengthens a case is an intermediary being present between the families. Purnima's case from Chapter 4 is a good example of this. Her father told a teacher about her statements of having been an incense maker, and the teacher and his brother-in-law located the previous personality's family. In such a situation, the intermediaries serve as additional witnesses to the child's statements, of course, but more importantly, they also serve as third parties who are more disinterested. Although the teacher and his brother-in-law were curious about whether Purnima's statements would match anyone's life in Kelaniya, they did not have the emotional investment in confirming the statements that a parent might.

Another feature that makes a case stronger is multiple witnesses. When written records are not available to show exactly what the child said, having ten witnesses who recall a child making a statement is obviously better than only having one. We always attempt to interview as many informants as possible. That is not to say that the memories of several individuals cannot mold together to form an inaccurate story, but the chances of inaccurate memory clearly decrease as more witnesses are available.

Occasionally, inaccurate statements by the child can even strengthen a case. In this situation, the child's version of events is different from the "official version," showing that his or her statements were not reconstructed after the fact. An example is the case of a boy named Ekkaphong that Dr. Keil and I investigated in Thailand. In that case, the previous personality was a young man in Ekkaphong's village who was accidentally killed while on a hunting outing with three friends. One of them dropped his rifle, which discharged and shot the young man. People in the village all identified a friend named Aet as the one whose rifle discharged, but Ekkaphong was so convinced that it was another friend named Phon that as a toddler, he tried to strangle Phon. He could not have obtained that belief from others in the village, since they thought that Aet was the one who dropped his rifle. It also makes no sense that the villagers would have falsely claimed to us that Ekkaphong had accused Phon incorrectly.

A case like this in which the subject and the previous personality were from the same village is not as impressive as when children report memories of the life of an individual who was completely unknown to their family. We see many cases of both types. In 971 cases from various cultures, 195 were same-family cases. In another sixty, the two families had a close association before the cases developed. In 115, they had a slight association. In ninety-three cases, the subject's family knew of the previous personality but had no association with him or her. Of the 971 cases, 508 were stranger cases. Of those, 239 were solved cases, 232 were unsolved, and a tentative identification had been made in the rest. Thus, we see a wide range of connections in the cases.

Considering the Explanations

Many of these cases are very similar to the cases of Indika and Purnima from the last chapter, only without the birthmarks. In some of them, fantasy along with coincidence might be used as an explanation if the child's statements are not too specific. When the child gives very specific details, however—for example, when Ratana Wongsombat stated the name of the previous personality, the places where she had lived, and even the fact that the previous personality's remains were scattered rather than buried—I think we can remove coincidence as a reasonable explanation.

One possibility is that the children learned about the previous life in normal ways. This can apply in the same-family cases and in ones where the child and the previous personality are from the same village. It gets less believable when we are talking about strangers who lived some distance away. The previous personality in Ratana's case lived for some time at a temple that Ratana's father attended, but since it was a very large temple on the other side of Bangkok from where Ratana lived, it is hard to see how Ratana could have learned about her. Many of the cases do not even have that kind of slight connection, so we cannot reasonably assume that the children somehow learned various personal details about their previous personalities by overhearing people talk about them.

In the case of Sujith Jayaratne, the previous personality lived in a village that was only seven miles from the child's home, so we might think that he had heard of the previous personality. When we consider, however, that the previous personality's village was a very different environment from the Colombo suburb where Sujith lived and that no one else in Sujith's family had ever heard of the previous personality, much less his father with a bad right eye, knowledge acquired through normal means does not seem a reasonable explanation either. When we add cases such as Kumkum Verma, whose previous personality lived twenty-five miles away, and Kemal Atasoy, the Turkish boy in the Introduction whose previous personality lived 500 miles away, it becomes quite unreasonable.

In such a situation, that problem is then compounded by the question of how, for instance, overhearing someone talk about a person in a market could lead children to identify with a deceased person who had led an ordinary life. On the whole, this explanation makes little sense for cases in which the families did not know the previous personalities and where we have no reason to think that the children would have even heard of them.

This brings us back to the possibility of faulty memory by informants. If we are going to use a normal explanation, we almost have to use this one for these cases. We can decide, for example, that Ratana did not actually say that the ashes of the previous personality were scattered rather than buried but that her father later recalled incorrectly that she did. Problems certainly exist with this explanation—the children have often made their claims repeatedly and multiple witnesses often recall the same specific claims—but without written documentation as evidence, we can try to place the blame on imperfect human memory.

This explanation fails when we consider cases in which a written record was made of the children's statements before the previous personality was identified. We cannot blame faulty memory in those cases, and as we have just seen, the other options for explaining the statements are limited. When Sujith Jayaratne said that the father of the previous personality was named Jamis and had a bad right eye, we can hardly think that all of his statements were due to coincidence. In fact, given the specificity of the statements in many of the cases, I would not have thought that any reasonable person would say that coincidence could be used to explain them, but Richard Wiseman, a psychologist at the University of Hertfordshire in Great Britain, has made that argument. He did an experiment in which he asked a few young children to make up stories about past lives, and he then tried to find a report of a death that matched the details that the child gave. His argument is that our cases could be like his, in which young children simply make up stories that in some ways match facts for a particular deceased person.

Dr. Wiseman has not published the results of his work, but he discussed it on two television documentaries in which we both participated. In his best case, a little girl named Molly told a story of a three-year-old girl named Katie, who was bitten by a monster and died. He then searched through newspaper archives and found a report of a three-year-old girl named Rosie who was kidnapped and killed. Molly's story had a number of features that were true for Rosie, including red hair, blue eyes, and a pink dress with flowers on it. Molly did not give a specific location but said that Katie had lived near the sea, which Rosie in fact did.

This case has obvious critical differences from ours. Along with the fact that Molly's story had the fantastic element of the monster, her description did not include a correct name of the child or a specific location, factors that are often crucial in our cases. While Dr. Wiseman's work may show that with a large enough archive, people can find some interesting things, it does not relate to cases of families going to specific places looking for specific people. In some ways, his study demonstrates that coincidence fails to explain important parts of the cases, even though his intention was to show the opposite.

This leaves us with out-and-out fraud as an explanation for the cases with written records. Of course, fraud could be used for the other cases we have talked about as well. Several problems exist with this option. First of all, we have no reason to question the integrity of the informants, who give us their time and attention while getting no benefit whatsoever from the investigations, and I think talking with these families about their experiences would convince any fair person that the people are being as straightforward and honest as they can be.

Second, in many of the cases, the families involved have no motive at all to perpetrate a fraud. Why would Sujith Jayaratne's mother convince him to pretend to have been a bootlegger? In Kumkum Verma's case, her father was not proud of her claim to have been in a lower class, and he never even allowed her to visit the previous family. Therefore, we have no reason to think that he coerced her into making her claims. Kemal Atasoy belonged to a prosperous family, and his parents would have absolutely no reason to encourage him to claim to have been a man who died fifty years before.

Third, in addition to the motive problems, engineering a fraud would not be feasible in many of the cases. The star of the show is usually a very young child, hardly the most reliable kind of person to use if you are trying to fool someone. Also, in many cases several people state that they have heard the children talk about the previous life over time, so we might have to decide that all of them would be involved in the fraud. The children are often said to recognize people or things from the previous life as well, and we can wonder how the parents would be able to help them do this.

In summary, the idea that a large number of these cases arise out of fraud does not really make sense, and were it not for the lack of alternative explanations, we would hardly even consider the possibility. In some ways, when people make an accusation of fraud without any evidence for it, they are admitting that they do not have a way of explaining a phenomenon. Labeling these cases as fraud means that we do not have an adequate normal explanation for them, but since we do not, we have to resort to fraud if we do not want to consider the paranormal explanations.

Regarding the paranormal explanations, ESP certainly seems worth considering, since the children appear to have knowledge about the previous life that they could not have obtained through normal means. As I discussed in Chapter 3, such an explanation presents several problems. Individuals who appear capable of extrasensory perception generally show abilities in more than one circumstance, except for cases in which two close family members appear at times to show a telepathic connection to each other. This situation is quite different, in that children who show no other paranormal abilities are able to give very specific details of the life of a deceased individual. The ESP explanation would also be in complete contrast to the subjective impression of the children, who believe they are recalling memories from the perspective of the deceased individual whose life they previously led.

Possession might also be able to explain the statements, but several factors argue against it. Although the children are often said to share some traits with the previous personality, no one says that they suddenly become the previous person. In addition, the statements are often intermittent. In many cases, the memories do not appear to be accessible to the children all the time, as they would if the previous personality had taken over the body. This might make us consider some type of temporary possession, except that the children do not lose the memories or personalities of their current life when they have the memories of the previous one. Lastly, the statements almost always start at a very early age. If these were examples of possession, then we might expect them to occur at various ages rather than only when the children are beginning to talk.

Reincarnation clearly explains the statements, as the children say that they remember previous lives. Several factors about the statements are odd, however, if reincarnation is the explanation. One, again, is that the memories do not appear to be accessible at all times to many of the children. If a child is a rebirth and is able to recall memories of the previous life, then we might think that he or she would be able to recall them all the time. While many of the children do not have access to the memories at all times, the other aspects of the cases show that the memories are more than just intermittent knowledge of paranormal material, as the ESP scenario would say. These "memories" are very meaningful to many of the children, and they certainly feel ownership of them, as if they are of prior events that the children experienced.

The statements often seem to represent a very incomplete description of the previous life. Some of the children, of course, appear to remember seemingly countless details of the previous life, but others report only a few. This might seem odd with respect to reincarnation until we compare it to memories from early in our lives. Early memories are often quite fuzzy, and at times, insignificant details can stand out as much as important events. Just as Kumkum Verma remembered that her father in the previous life lived near mango orchards, we might recall a particular feature about a place or perhaps a person we knew. The children talk about people and events from near the end of the previous life, because those memories are less distant than earlier ones.

The statements the children make remain the core of the cases. As we have seen, the children are often said to possess knowledge about a deceased individual that their parents feel they could not have obtained by normal means. Though this knowledge provides the strongest evidence in the cases, the other features we study are important in showing that this phenomenon is about more than just the statements. Behaviors like Sujith's phobia of trucks that began in infancy and his desire for alcohol and tobacco clearly demand an explanation. We will look more at such behaviors in the next chapter.

CHAPTER 6

Unusual Behaviors

Kendra Carter, a girl who lives in Florida, was four and a half years old when she went to her first swimming lesson with a coach named Ginger. She immediately jumped into Ginger's lap and acted very lovingly toward her. When Ginger had to cancel a lesson three weeks later, Kendra sobbed uncontrollably. When she was able to have a lesson soon after, she was very happy and began talking about Ginger all the time.

A few weeks later, Kendra began saying that Ginger's baby had died and that Ginger had been sick and had pushed her baby out. When her mother asked her how she knew these things, Kendra replied, "I'm the baby that was in her tummy." At that point, Kendra had only seen Ginger at their lessons, and her mother knew that the two of them had never been alone. Kendra described an abortion, saying that Ginger had allowed a bad man to pull her out and that she had tried to hang on but could not. She described being scared in a dark and cold place afterwards. Kendra's mother eventually found out from Ginger that she had in fact had an abortion nine years before Kendra was born when she was unmarried, sick, and dealing with anorexia nervosa.

Kendra began saying that she would die, because Ginger had been unable to deliver her. She said, "I have to die, and I won't come back this time." This fear of dying became so severe that Kendra's mother took her to a therapist, who suggested a ceremony in which Kendra would be "born" to Ginger. Following this, her fear of dying seemed to resolve.

Even though Ginger was often cool toward her, Kendra began being very bubbly and happy when she was with Ginger but quiet and withdrawn otherwise. Her mother allowed her to spend more and more time with Ginger. Eventually, Ginger set up a room for Kendra in her home, and Kendra spent three nights a week there. Kendra's absences were hard for her mother, but she permitted them, because Kendra's wish to be with Ginger was so intense.

Unfortunately, Ginger and Kendra's mother eventually had a falling-out, and Ginger said that she did not want to see Kendra anymore. Following this, Kendra did not speak for four and a half months. She showed no interest in activities, ate little, and slept a lot. At the end of that time, Ginger met with Kendra for two hours. During this meeting, Kendra talked again for the first time when she told Ginger that she loved her. Ginger began calling Kendra again, but Kendra did not feel comfortable going to her home. Kendra slowly began talking more, and she began participating more in activities.

Kendra's mother found all of this very troubling. Her daughter's struggle with the situation upset her, and the possibility of reincarnation troubled her as well. She attended a conservative Christian church, and she felt that she was committing a sin by merely buying a book on reincarnation during Kendra's troubles. She decided that perhaps Kendra's spirit had been looking for another body after Ginger's abortion, but she did not accept the idea that reincarnation is a process that normally occurs.

This case presents us with a number of perplexing questions. Why would a four-year-old girl think that she had been involved in an abortion? What caused her to develop the idea of reincarnation when she was being raised by a mother who could not even consider the possibility? And why did she become so emotionally attached to a woman who was often not very warm toward her?

Surviving Emotions

The depression that Kendra suffered is an example of the emotional component that is present in many of these cases. To hear of children crying for years for their family to take them to their previous parents until the family finally relents is not unusual. Other children can show emotional outbursts for a very short time, just as Olivia in the last chapter became distraught during the one time that she talked about losing her family. In addition to the longing for the previous family that many of the children demonstrate, some show emotions toward individual members of that family that would be appropriate for the relationship that the previous personality had with that person. For instance, the children are often deferential toward a husband or parents of the previous personality, but they may be bossy toward younger siblings, even if the siblings are adults at the time that the young subjects meet them.

Sukla Gupta in India is another subject who showed great emotion. She was less than two years old when she began the habit of cradling a block of wood or a pillow and calling it "Minu." She said that Minu was her daughter, and during the next three years, she gradually spoke more about a previous life. She gave a number of details, including the name and section of a village eleven miles away. A woman there who had an infant daughter named Minu had died six years before Sukla was born and was identified as the previous personality. When Sukla was five years old, her family went to meet the family of the previous personality. She cried when she met Minu, then eleven years old, and she appeared affectionate and maternal toward her. At one point, one of the previous personality's cousins tested Sukla by telling her falsely that Minu was sick with a high fever. Sukla began to weep, and she could not be comforted for some time. In another instance, Minu actually was sick, and when Sukla learned the news, she began crying and demanded to be taken to her. She remained agitated until the next day when her family took her to see Minu, who had improved by then.

Sukla also appeared deferential toward the previous personality's husband. After they met, she longed for him to visit her. He did so weekly for about a year, until his second wife complained about the visits, and he began to visit less frequently. Sukla talked less about the previous life after the age of seven, and she also gradually lost her feelings of attachment toward the previous personality's husband and Minu. By the time she was an early teen, she complained that they were pestering her when they came to visit.

The feelings of the subjects do not always diminish over time, and at least one subject, Maung Aye Kyaw in Myanmar, grew up to marry the widow of the previous personality. The longevity of the feelings often depends on how much contact the families have after they initially meet. Many of the families become quite friendly, with frequent visits at least initially, but some are resistant. This resistance may relate to the previous family's occasional concern that the subject's family is looking for gifts from them or the feeling of the subject's family that the child may become too attached to the previous one. Significant socioeconomic distance between the families can also produce awkwardness at times.

Subjects can also show very negative feelings toward figures in the life of the previous personality. I have already mentioned the case of Ekkaphong, who tried to strangle the man he thought was responsible for the death of the previous personality. Other subjects have shown either similar anger or fear toward the individuals that they said killed the previous personality. Bongkuch Promsin, a case I will discuss in more detail in Chapter 8, said that he would kill the previous personality's murderers when he grew up, but his threats fortunately lessened as he became older. Maung Aye Kyaw, the subject who married the widow of his previous personality, threw stones at one of the men he said had killed him in his previous life, and other subjects have done the same with the killers or alleged killers of their previous personalities.

Fear-death Experiences

Many of the subjects show a phobia that relates to the mode of death of the previous personality. In cases in which the previous personality died by unnatural means, more than 35 percent of the subjects show phobias related to the previous life. They seem particularly common in drowning cases, appearing in thirty-one out of fifty-three cases. We might speculate that this increased frequency could be because drowning victims spend more time in the process of dying than individuals who are killed in an automobile accident or shot to death.

These phobias can appear when the children are very young. Shamlinie Prema, whom I mentioned in Chapter 1, showed an intense fear of being immersed in water from the time she was an infant. Three people had to hold her down for her baths. Beginning at the age of six months, she also showed a great fear of buses. When she became old enough to talk, she reported memories of the life of a girl in the nearby village of Galtudawa, and, in fact, her first words were "Galtudawa mother." The girl in Galtudawa was eleven years old when she died one and a half years before Shamlinie was born. She had been walking along a narrow road when a bus came by. When she tried to step out of its way, she fell into a flooded patty field next to the road and drowned.

Shamlinie began getting over her fear of being bathed when she was three years old, and the fear had completely resolved by the time she was four. Her fear of buses lasted longer, until she was at least five and a half years old, which was about the time that she stopped talking spontaneously about the previous life. Shamlinie's behavior was similar to that of Sujith Jayaratne, the boy in the previous chapter who showed a fear of trucks, and even of the word *lorry,* before he was a year old and before he related details of the life of a man who died when a truck ran over him.

In general, as the children grow older, the phobias tend to diminish along with the statements about the previous life. Exceptions do exist in which older children still show a fear even though they apparently no longer have memories of the events from the previous life that seemed to be connected to it.

Unacquired Tastes

Sujith Jayaratne's case demonstrates another unusual behavior we have found in some of these cases—interest in addictive substances that the previous personality used. Sujith displayed a desire to indulge in alcohol and cigarettes, and a number of the other subjects have as well. Though not common, thirty-four of the children out of 1,100 cases showed an unusual desire for alcohol or tobacco that was consistent with the previous personality's tastes.

Some of the children show unusual food habits and preferences, which can be problematic for some of the Indian children who report memories of lives in higher castes than their own. Jasbir Singh, an Indian boy, reported memories of the life of a Brahmin, a higher caste than that of his family. He refused to eat his family's food, and a kind Brahmin neighbor agreed to prepare food for him in the Brahmin manner. This went on for more than a year and a half until the boy finally relented to eating his family's food.

In some cases, the subject may be the only person in the family to enjoy a food for which the previous personality had a particular fondness. This is especially noticeable in the international cases. Dr. Stevenson, with some recent additions by Dr. Keil, has collected two dozen cases of Burmese children who reported being Japanese soldiers killed in Burma during World War II. None of the children has given enough specific details to identify a previous personality in Japan, but the children's behavior has often been quite distinctive, including food preferences. A number of these children complain about the spicy Burmese food and prefer sweet foods and raw or partially cooked fish.

The case of Ma Tin Aung Myo, born in 1953, is a good example. During her pregnancy, her mother dreamed three times that a Japanese army cook whom she had known during the Japanese army's occupation of Burma followed her and said that he wanted to come and stay with her family. When Ma Tin Aung Myo was four years old, she was walking with her father one day when she became very upset as an airplane flew overhead. After that, she cried every time a plane flew over, a behavior she showed for a number of years. She said that she was afraid that the planes would shoot her. Around that time, she began saying that she longed for Japan, and she gradually told the story of being a Japanese soldier who was killed by machine-gun fire from a low-flying plane while he was stationed in her family's village.

In addition to her phobia of planes and her longing for Japan, Ma Tin Aung Myo complained of the hot Burmese climate. She also did not like spicy Burmese food and preferred to eat sweet foods, and she liked fish, particularly half-cooked fish, as a young child. She used words that her family could not understand, but since no one around her knew Japanese, we have no way of determining if these might have been Japanese words.

Ma Tin Aung Myo did not show one feature that the children in a number of these Burmese-Japanese cases have shown, which is a great reluctance to wear traditional Burmese attire. Burmese men and women generally wear *longyis,* a garment similar to an ankle-length skirt, with shirts or blouses, but a number of the children have insisted on wearing trousers instead, as Japanese men would do.

These cases of Burmese children who claim to remember lives as Japanese soldiers are similar to the unsolved case of Carl Edon, a British boy who seemed to remember the life of a German pilot in World War II. Born in 1972, he began saying, "I crashed a plane through a window" when he was two years old. He gradually added details about having been on a bombing mission over England when he crashed. When he became able to draw, he drew swastikas and eagles and, later, the panel of a cockpit. He also demonstrated the Nazi salute and the goose-step march of German soldiers. He said that he wanted to live in Germany. He, unlike the other members of his family, liked to eat sausages and thick soups.

In addition to behaviors indicating a difference in nationality, some cases show behaviors indicative of a class or caste difference. I have already mentioned Jasbir Singh, who refused to eat non-Brahmin food. He also used terms for some objects that those in higher classes generally used. He continued to think of himself as a Brahmin as he grew older. As an adult, he had trouble getting a job that he did not consider beneath him. Some children have also shown unusual behaviors in the opposite direction. Swaran Lata, a girl who was born into a Brahmin family, reported memories of being a sweepress, a woman who sweeps streets and cleans latrines. She tended to be quite dirty and cleaned up the stools of younger children. She also resisted going to school when she was young by saying, "We are sweepers. Nobody studies in our family, and I never sent my children to school."

The Play's the Thing

A prominent area of behavior in these cases is that of the children's play. In Chapter 1, I mentioned Parmod Sharma, a boy who played at being a biscuit shopkeeper with such persistence that his schooling suffered. Such play is common, with at least a quarter of the subjects showing themes in their play that seem connected to the previous life. This often involves play mimicking the occupation of the previous personality as in Parmod's case, but other forms occur as well. I have described the case of Sukla Gupta, who would cradle a piece of wood or a pillow in her arms and call it "Minu," the name of the previous personality's daughter.

Some children act out the way the previous personality died. Maung Myint Soe, a boy in Myanmar who reported memories of a man who drowned on a ferryboat, would from time to time act out a scene in which he pretended to attempt an escape from a sinking boat. Ramez Shams of Lebanon reenacted the suicide of the previous personality by repeatedly putting a stick under his chin while pretending that it was a rifle. Such play is rare in our cases but when present is very similar to the play of children who have survived a major traumatic event in this lifetime. Those children may show behavior known as post-traumatic play in which they reenact the scene with dolls or other objects.

If our subjects are in fact cases of reincarnation, then this play, along with the phobias that some of the subjects show toward the mode of death of the previous personality, demonstrates that the emotional trauma of a violent death can carry over from one life to the next. Though this is not surprising in some ways and is consistent with birthmarks arising from fatal injuries in the previous life, the idea that those who experience difficult deaths have trouble putting the trauma immediately behind them is a sobering one.

Changing Sexes

In the sex-change cases, cases in which the child claims to remember the life of a member of the opposite sex, we have observed cross-gender behavior. In one series of sex-change cases, twenty-one out of thirty-four cases (62 percent), showed behavior that was appropriate for the opposite sex. Examples include Kloy Matwiset, the boy in Chapter 4 born with a birthmark on the back of his neck that matched an experimental mark made on his grandmother's body. He showed a number of cross-gender behaviors, including saying that he wanted to be a girl, sitting down to urinate, and repeatedly wearing his mother's lipstick, earrings, and dresses.

The other sex-change case I have described is Ma Tin Aung Myo, the Burmese girl who reported memories of the life of a Japanese soldier killed in Burma during World War II. She also showed a strong identification as a male. When she was young, she played with boys, and, in particular, she liked to pretend to be a soldier. She said that she wanted to be a soldier and asked her parents to buy toy guns for her. She also insisted on wearing boys' clothes, and this produced a crisis when school authorities demanded that she come to school dressed as a girl. She refused and dropped out of school at the age of eleven. As a young adult, she continued to identify herself as a male, and she preferred that people address her using a male honorific instead of a female one. Dr. Stevenson last saw her family when she was twenty-seven years old. At that point, she was living with her steady girlfriend in another town. Her family reported that she still talked about wanting to join the army and continued to dress as a male.

Before we consider what could lead to this cross-gender behavior, we need to look at current thinking about gender identity disorder in general. It is a disorder in which children show an identification with the opposite sex and discomfort with their own sex. Though quite a bit of research has been done, its cause is still largely unknown. A number of biological and psychological factors are thought to be required to interact during a critical time period to produce the disorder. Some have speculated that sex hormones during pregnancy could be involved, but little direct evidence is available to support that.

Most of the research that has been done on gender identity disorder has been with boys. Though rare among all children, it is much more common in boys than in girls. In that research, no clear evidence exists that mothers of boys with the disorder want to have a girl more than other mothers, but in some cases, their disappointment about not having had a girl may affect how they relate to their sons. Other factors that may be associated include psychological disturbance in the parents, anxiety in many of the children about separating from their parents, and such psychological issues as a distant father-son relationship and a mother's perception that females are more nurturing than males.

In Kloy's case, his parents thought that he was his grandmother reborn because of the birthmark on his neck, and we might wonder if they unconsciously steered his behavior to be feminine because of that, even though they said that they did not talk to him about the previous life and that they discouraged his cross-gender behaviors. The same scenario occurred in the case of Ma Tin Aung Myo. Her mother's dreams about the Japanese soldier may have at least raised the possibility in her mind that he would be reborn as her child, but she did not intentionally encourage Ma Tin Aung Myo to want to be a boy.

Whether a mother's wishes or expectations could exert a significant influence over a child's subsequent gender identity is not clear. Cases have recently been reported in which boys were raised as girls after they had accidents as infants in which they lost their penises. In one case, the patient did develop a female gender identity but also had a childhood history of being a "tomboy" and developed a bisexual orientation while being mainly attracted to women. In the others, the patients developed male gender identities despite their parents' best efforts to raise them as girls, so we have little reason to think that the parents in our cases, because of their past-life beliefs, could have unconsciously interacted with their children in ways that produced the gender identity disorder.

The case of Erin Jackson, an American whose Protestant parents did not believe in reincarnation before the case developed, is a strong example. When she was three years old, she talked about having been a boy and described a life with a stepmother and a brother, James, who only liked to wear black. She did not give any direct details of when that life took place, but she appeared to be remembering a life in the distant past, because she would say things like, "It was lots better when there were horses. These cars are awful. They've just ruined everything."

Erin sometimes said that she wished she were a boy, and she insisted on dressing as one when she was little. This extended to bathing suits. When Erin would only wear the bottom of a two-piece suit, her mother learned to buy one-piece suits. As Erin grew older, she would wear a dress perhaps three times a year, and then only if it did not have lace or ruffles.

We can consider several possibilities to explain cross-gender behavior in our cases. One is that the cross-gender behavior and the past-life claims only occur together by coincidence. Arguing against that are the dozens of cases we have that involve the combination of a gender identity disorder, which is a rare disorder, with claims of having been a member of the opposite sex. With so many cases, we must conclude that the two are connected.

We might like to suppose that the cross-gender behavior displayed by Kloy Matwiset and Ma Tin Aung Myo came because their parents thought they were the rebirths of members of the opposite sex, but we cannot do so in Erin's case. Her parents did not expect her to be the rebirth of anyone, and her talk of having been a boy, which occurred in combination with her boyish behavior, obviously came as a complete surprise. We might decide that her wish to be a boy happened first and that she then added a fantasy of having been a boy in a previous life. Such an explanation for these cases—that the gender identity disorder leads to the past-life claims—does not apply to Kloy's case because his parents thought that he might be his grandmother reborn before he ever had a gender identity. These cases put us in a bind when we look for a normal explanation. In Erin's case, we might like to blame the cross-gender wishes for producing the past-life beliefs, while in Kloy's case, we would be more inclined to blame the past-life beliefs for producing cross-gender behavior.

Since the connection between the cross-gender behavior and the belief that the child had a previous life as a member of the opposite sex can occur in either order, one of them does not always cause the other. How, then, do we explain the behavior? The final normal explanation would be that the families have exaggerated the extent of the cross-gender behaviors because of their belief that the child had a previous life as a member of the opposite sex. This seems quite unlikely in cases as extreme as that of Ma Tin Aung Myo, who once told Dr. Stevenson and his interpreter that they could kill her by any means they wanted if they could guarantee that she would be reborn as a male. Dr. Stevenson noted that they had no wish to carry out the former and no power to implement the latter.

Twins Who Remember

Subjects who are identical twins offer a unique contribution to our understanding of the behavior of these children. In Chapter 4, I discussed Indika Ishwara, an identical twin in Sri Lanka who described the life of a boy who had died of encephalitis at the age of ten. Indika's twin brother, Kakshappa, also claimed to remember a previous life. He spoke of it before Indika did, claiming that the police had shot him. Judging from other statements he made, his family decided he was talking about the life of an insurgent who died during an uprising in Sri Lanka in 1971. The family laughed at his claims, and he soon stopped making them.

The twins showed some differences in temperament and behavior. Indika, who remembered the life of a schoolboy, tended to be gentle and calm, while Kakshappa, who recalled the life of an insurgent, presented himself as being tough and tended to be hostile and aggressive. Indika was religious as a young child, as his previous personality was, but Kakshappa was not. Indika was more intelligent and was interested and successful in his schoolwork, while Kakshappa did poorly in school. Indika's features even matched those of the boy whose life he appeared to remember. The twins' parents noted that the differences in their personalities lessened as they grew older.

How do we explain the differences that they showed initially? Their statements about the previous lives seem to have come too late to cause their parents to interact with them in a manner that would produce the differences. As some twins develop, they show contrasting interests that emphasize each child's uniqueness. In this case, the way that the differences began early and lessened over time is more consistent with an inborn factor than with an environmental one, but we cannot use this normal explanation of inborn differences since the boys are identical twins. If the differences that were present initially were due to carryover from the previous lives, then the fact that they lessened suggests either that the effect from the previous lives naturally dissipated over time or that experiences in the current life gradually had a larger and larger effect on the boys.

The Case of the Pollock Twins

Gillian and Jennifer Pollock, born in Hexham, Northumberland, England, in 1958, form another interesting case involving identical twins. Their older sisters, Joanna and Jacqueline, had been killed a year and a half before the twins were born when a car struck them as they walked to church. When their mother became pregnant with Gillian and Jennifer, their father, who, unlike their mother, believed in reincarnation, stated confidently that the two deceased girls were going to be reborn as twins, despite the obstetrician's statement that only one fetus was present.

When the twins were born, their parents noticed two birthmarks on Jennifer, the younger twin, that matched two marks that had been present on Jacqueline, the younger of the deceased girls. One matched a birthmark that Jacqueline had on her hip, and the other matched a scar that Jacqueline had received when she fell on a bucket and cut her forehead. Gillian, the older of the twins, had no birthmarks.

The family moved from Hexham when the twins were nine months old. When they were three years old, they began talking about their older sisters, and in particular, their mother overheard them several times discussing details of the accident in which their sisters were killed. In addition, their parents had packed the toys of the older girls away when they were killed, but later got two dolls out. When the twins saw them, Gillian claimed the doll that had belonged to Joanna, the oldest sister, while Jennifer claimed Jacqueline's. They said that Santa Claus had given them the dolls, and their older sisters, in fact, had received them as Christmas presents. In addition, when Gillian saw a toy clothes wringer that had been a Christmas gift of Joanna's, she said, "Look! There is my toy wringer," and stated that Santa Claus had given it to her.

One day, Gillian pointed to the birthmark on Jennifer's forehead and said, "That is the mark Jennifer got when she fell on a bucket." While Jennifer had not had an accident producing the mark, Jacqueline had indeed fallen on a bucket, receiving an injury that required stitches and produced a permanent scar. At another time, when their father was painting, he wore a smock their mother had previously used when the older girls were alive. Jennifer saw it and asked, "Why are you wearing Mummy's coat?" When her father asked her how she knew that it was her mother's, she correctly responded that her mother had worn the smock when delivering milk.

When the twins were four years old, the family returned to Hexham for the first time to visit for the day. As the family walked along a road near a park where the older girls had frequently played, the twins said that they wanted to go across the road to the swings in the park. Neither the swings nor even the park was visible when they said this.

In addition to Jennifer's birthmarks and the twins' statements, the girls also demonstrated behaviors consistent with the lives of their older sisters. Gillian tended to "mother" Jennifer, who accepted her leadership, just as Joanna had tended to mother Jacqueline, who was five years younger. In addition, when the twins learned to write at around the age of four and a half, Gillian immediately held a pencil between her thumb and fingers, but Jennifer held a pencil upright in her fist. Jacqueline, who was six years old when she was killed, had persisted in holding her pencil this way despite her teacher's best efforts to get her to hold it properly. Jennifer eventually learned the correct grip when she was seven years old, but she lapsed into using the previous one at times even as an adult. Since she and Gillian were identical twins in the same environment, this difference is puzzling.

The obvious weakness of this case is the father's conviction before the twins were even born that they were the reincarnation of their sisters. It may have increased the connections he thought he observed and even the twins' propensity to talk about the sisters, though it clearly did not cause Jennifer's birthmarks. The twins stopped making any statements about their sisters at the age of seven. Their mother, who had not believed in reincarnation initially, by then was convinced by their statements, birthmarks, and behaviors that they were their deceased sisters reborn, sharing the belief that their father had voiced while they were still in the womb.

Explaining the behavioral differences in our identical twin subjects is a significant challenge. The two cases I have presented show that not only do the identical twin subjects show these differences, but the differences are quite consistent with the previous lives the children describe. These cases of twins bring up the issue of what contributes to personality. In general, scientists have assumed that individual differences of any kind are due to genetic or environmental factors. In child development, the degree of influence of genetics versus environment is controversial, but temperament is one useful concept of the biological factors that contribute to personality differences. Temperament refers to how individuals perform behaviors, as opposed to why they perform them, which is motivation, or what they perform, which is ability. Biological factors like temperament interact with environmental factors to produce the various personality differences in individuals. The temperament shown in early childhood tends to be stable, but as a child ages, temperament characteristics can change.

When we consider identical twins, we are dealing with two individuals who have the same genetic makeup. As expected, identical twins show a great deal of similarity in temperament, much more so than fraternal twins, but the similarity is not 100 percent. Since temperament is thought to be a biological dimension, the differences in identical twins become difficult to explain, because their genetic makeup is identical.

To explain personality differences in identical twins, we

must consider environmental factors. Most twins have the same general environment, but perhaps parents respond uniquely to each twin and produce differences that way. In addition, these cases suggest that, along with heredity and environment, we should consider the idea that differences may be caused by what the consciousness brings to a new life.

Emotional Consequences

The various behaviors in this chapter are evidence supporting the reincarnation explanation and indicate that more than just memories may be able to survive from one life to the next. Emotions, attachments, fears, addictions, likes and dislikes, and even identification with a particular country and with a gender may be able to carry over from one life to the next. If reincarnation does occur, emotions as well as memories survive.

The emotions do not necessarily continue throughout this life. The behaviors often persist past the point when the children stop talking about a previous life, but they generally fade away over time. Most of the subjects in sex-change cases eventually take on a gender identity consistent with their anatomical sex. Ma Tin Aung Myo, who showed a male gender identity as an adult, was an exception. We have plenty of cases where the emotions and behaviors did not fade away, but given the complications that can occur in such a situation, perhaps letting them go when they will is the best thing to do.

Along these lines, Kendra's case is a cautionary tale, as it shows the difficulty that can develop from apparent memories and demonstrates that talk about a previous life is not fun and games for the children involved. Kendra became extremely attached to her coach Ginger, and she was devastated when the attachment was ultimately disrupted. She would have been better off if she had not held the belief that she had been in Ginger's womb. Dr. Stevenson has written about the suffering in other cases as well. As he points out, many of the children suffer tremendously, because they feel separated from the families to which they feel such a strong attachment. Their parents, likewise, have to deal with a child who in many ways is rejecting them. On a more optimistic note, he also points out that later in life, benefits can occur from the apparent memories, as some subjects have talked of using their past mistakes as a guide to improving their behavior in the current life. He cites Bishen Chand Kapoor, whom I mentioned in Chapter 3, whose previous personality murdered a man when he saw him leaving the apartment of a prostitute whom the previous personality considered reserved for himself. Bishen Chand said that reflecting on the negative aspects of his previous life had helped make him a better person.

Others have shown a detachment from problems in the current life or a lack of any fear of death. Marta Lorenz, a girl in Brazil who made voluminous statements about the life of a friend of her mother's, experienced the death of a sister, Emilia. When another sister worried during a rainstorm that Emilia would get wet in her grave, Marta responded, "Emilia is not in the cemetery. She is in a safer and better place than this one where we are; her soul never can be wet." Similarly, when a family friend grieving the death of her father said that the dead never return, Marta replied, "Don't say that. I died also and look, I am living again."

Dr. Stevenson has also written about the relief that can occur after the children meet the previous personality's family for the first time. The children often seem better able to integrate the memories from the past life with the circumstances of their present life after the meeting, and the intensity of their emotions about the past life often lessens. Kendra's case points out that relationships individuals have in this life are different from those they may have had in a past life. Even if we accept that her consciousness was a part of Ginger's aborted fetus, that does not mean that they are mother and daughter in this life. They clearly are not, but Kendra seemed confused about this. She spoke of having two mothers and spent a good deal of time with Ginger. In such a situation, the child needs to understand that relationships from a past life are in the past and not the present, and the meeting with the previous family often seems to facilitate such an understanding.

In some ways, Asian parents may have an advantage in this situation compared to Western ones. In our cases in Asia, the parents usually accept a child's claims about a past life, even if they try to get the child to stop making them. They can address emotional issues directly and tell their children that though they had different parents in the past life, their current parents are the ones they have this time around. Western parents, on the other hand, may be puzzled by their child's statements and not know how to respond. They may ignore the statements, or they may say that the child is lying or pretending. None of these responses is satisfying to the child, and none sends the same message the Asian parents often convey. Kendra's mother eventually accepted that her spirit may have once inhabited Ginger's fetus, but unfortunately, Kendra showed little ability to place that relationship in the past.

Many of the Asian subjects have trouble letting go of the past as well, but they often seem to be able to do so more easily after they meet the previous family. Such a meeting validates their memories, yet the children understand that they will continue to live with their current family. A definite message that the past is in the past may be helpful, and this can be a hard message for Western parents to convey if they cannot accept the possibility, as Kendra's mother was able to do, that their children's claims about the past may be true.

Considering the Explanations

Developing a normal explanation for the behaviors can be difficult. In some cases, we may want to use the fantasy explanation and say that the children's behavior comes from their false identification with a previous personality. Where would such a fantasy come from in the first place? We might blame cultural factors for the cases in Asia, but we can hardly do so in the case of Kendra Carter, whose mother was appalled by the idea of reincarnation. Similarly, Erin Jackson, who showed cross-gender behavior, had Protestant parents who did not believe in reincarnation when her symptoms started. In addition, do we have a reasonable explanation for what would lead Burmese children to identify themselves as Japanese soldiers or a British boy to identify himself as a German pilot as Carl Edon did?

Regarding the emotions specifically, we might like to suppose that the ones that the children show when they interact with family members of the previous personality are the result of their fantasy that they were previously related. This idea gets less likely when we look at the longing that some of the children express before they ever meet the other family.

A case such as Sukla Gupta, who mothered objects she called "Minu" before other details she gave led to the identification of a previous personality who had an infant daughter named Minu, stretches this idea to the limit. How did she develop this intense longing for Minu before anyone located the previous family? We can conclude that this was a remarkable coincidence, that Sukla had somehow learned numerous details about the life of a woman who died in another village six years before she was born, or that the family falsely remembered her cradling "Minu." Regardless of which of these we choose, we also have to deal with the strong attachment that Sukla showed to the real Minu after they met. Can we really conclude that all of this emotion came from a child's fantasy?

The same question comes up when we look at Kendra's case. We can understand a young girl becoming attached to her swimming coach, but her attachment was so immediate and so intense that it would be highly unusual under any circumstances. To that, we then have to add that the girl, whose mother and church found the concept of reincarnation to be abhorrent, imagined that she had previously been the coach's aborted fetus. In her case, since the attachment seemed to come either simultaneously with or slightly prior to the reincarnation claim, we cannot realistically decide that it came from a reincarnation fantasy. Can we say the reverse—that the reincarnation fantasy came from the extreme attachment that she felt—when we know that no one in her environment had a belief in reincarnation? Even if we do, that means that in some cases we think that a fantasy produced the attachment, with Sukla being an example, while in others like Kendra's, the attachment led to the fantasy.

Complicating both of these scenarios is the intensity of the emotions that some of the children show. A child like Kendra, who did not speak for four months after her purported previous mother cut off contact, is not engaging in a childish game of make-believe. Similar examples abound, like Ekkaphong, who tried to strangle the man he thought had killed him in a previous life, and of course Sukla, who wept when she heard that Minu was sick. In addition, in some of the cases of gender confusion, the cross-gender behaviors persist into adulthood, so they hardly seem part of a child's fantasy play.

Let us look at phobias. Shamlinie Prema and Sujith Jayaratne both showed phobias as babies. Shamlinie's intense fear of being immersed in water from the time she was an infant obviously could not have grown out of a fantasy about a past life. We might want to use the faulty memory explanation here, so we would say that after the children talked about previous lives, their parents recalled their earlier behaviors as being more extreme than they really were. The same is true for the precocious interest in addictive substances and the unusual food habits that some of the parents report that their children show. Refuting this is Jasbir Singh's case, since we cannot say that his parents exaggerated his refusal to eat their food after they had to get a Brahmin neighbor to prepare food for him for a year and a half. Overall, we have enough witnesses and enough cases in which the behaviors persisted to say that some of the children definitely show behaviors that at least appear to be connected with the past-life memories they claim to have.

And so it goes with efforts to explain the behaviors the

children often show in these cases. We may be able to piece together a normal explanation for individual cases, even if, at times, it seems rather convoluted, but the explanations do not hold up when we look at the phenomena as a group. In some cases, the past-life claims come first, and in some, the behaviors come first. While the behaviors are often extreme enough to make a normal explanation difficult in either case, having a single explanation that encompasses both situations and provides an overall interpretation of the phenomena is essentially impossible, and the explanation for one group of cases is the opposite of the explanation for the other group.

As for the paranormal explanations, ESP does not do a good job of explaining these cases. It only works if we say that when the children acquire the knowledge through ESP, they think that they are experiencing memories. This mistaken impression then causes them to develop the emotions and behaviors. This is convoluted, obviously; but worse, some of the behaviors, such as the phobias, often exist well before the children make statements about the previous life. Perhaps we could argue that the children acquire the knowledge of the previous lives as infants, and while this seems odd, it is at least conceivable.

Possession seems to do a better job of explaining the emotions and behaviors than ESP does. If the previous consciousness has taken over the body of the child, then we might well expect that the child would show such traits. The weakness of this argument is that we would have to say the possession occurred almost at birth, since some of the behavioral traits start at such an early age. Therefore, it would be hard to justify this as a better explanation than reincarnation.

Reincarnation, again, does provide an explanation for the

emotions and behaviors. In fact, they show that if reincarnation is the explanation for the cases, then it involves more than just memories. It encompasses a more complete continuance from the previous life, as emotional connections, fears, and likes and dislikes are all part of the consciousness that moves on to the next life.

These behavioral features demonstrate that the children's past-life claims are very meaningful to them. Anyone who thinks that they are just a silly game of make-believe or something that children say to satisfy their parents' beliefs in reincarnation should remember Kendra, a small American child who was unable to speak for months after the woman that she remembered as her mother rejected her.

CHAPTER 7

Recognizing Familiar Faces

Sam Taylor is a boy from Vermont who was born a year and a half after his paternal grandfather died. When Sam was one and a half years old, his father was changing his diaper one day when Sam told him, "When I was your age, I used to change your diapers." After his mother saw the puzzled look on his father's face as he brought Sam out of his room, they discussed the comment, which they both found odd. Neither had ever given reincarnation much thought. Though Sam's mother was the daughter of a Southern Baptist minister, his parents were not religious.

Following that incident, Sam gradually began saying that he had been his grandfather. He also said, "I used to be big, and now I'm small." While his father was initially skeptical about such a possibility, his mother was more open to the idea, and she began asking him questions about the life of his paternal grandfather. At one point, she and Sam were talking about the fact that his grandmother had taken care of his grandfather before he died. Sam's mother asked him what his grandmother made every day for his grandfather to drink, and Sam correctly said that she had made milkshakes and that she had made them in a machine in the kitchen. He got up to show her the food processor on the kitchen counter. When his mother showed him the blender in the pantry and asked if he meant that his grandmother had made the milkshakes with it, he said no and pointed out the food processor instead. In fact, his grandmother had made milkshakes for his grandfather in the food processor. She then had a series of strokes after the death of his grandfather, and Sam had never seen her make milkshakes for anyone.

At another time, Sam's mother asked him if he had had any brothers or sisters when he lived before. He answered, "Yeah, I had a sister. She turned into a fish." When she asked him who turned her into a fish, he said, "Some bad guys. She died. You know what, when we die, God lets us come back again. I used to be big, and now I'm a kid again." The sister of Sam's grandfather, in fact, had been killed some sixty years before. Her husband killed her while she was sleeping, rolled her body up in a blanket, and dumped it in the bay.

At other times, Sam correctly said that his grandfather's favorite place in the home was the garage where he worked on "inventions" and that Sam's father had a small steering wheel of his own when they rode in the car. When his father was a boy, he had a toy steering wheel that attached to the dashboard of a car by suction cups.

When Sam was four and a half years old, his grandmother died. His father flew out to her home to take care of her belongings and returned with a box of family photographs. Sam's parents had not had any pictures of his father's family before then. When his mother spread them out on the coffee table one night, Sam came over and began pointing to the pictures of his grandfather and saying, "That's me!" When he saw a snapshot that showed a car without any people, he said "Hey! That's my car!" This was a picture of the first new car that his grandfather ever purchased, a 1949 Pontiac that was very special to him.

His mother gave Sam a class picture from when his grandfather was in grammar school. The picture showed twenty-seven children, sixteen of them boys. Sam ran his finger over the faces, stopped it on his grandfather's face and said, "That's me."

His father says that Sam's grandfather did not communicate very well about emotional issues with his sons, particularly when they were adults. Sam's father let his own father know how he felt about him, but his father had great difficulty reciprocating. He feels that if his father has come back through Sam, then his deceased father is reaching out to return his love. Sam's father is very open with all of his children, and he and Sam seem to have a very good relationship.

Sam was thought to recognize someone or something from the previous life, identifying the previous personality, his grandfather, in pictures and also pointing out a picture of his grandfather's car. This is similar to the reports in many of our cases of children recognizing family members of the previous personality.

The recognitions in the cases fall into several categories. The first type involves uncontrolled recognitions. In these, the families attempt to test the child to see if he or she can recognize previous family members or belongings, but they do not conduct the tests under the controlled conditions that we would favor. Though the tests usually involve recognizing people, locations are sometimes involved. Witnesses in those cases say that the children led the way to the home of the previous personality or that they noted changes in buildings or landscapes that had occurred after the death of the previous personality.

Unfortunately, the conditions that the families frequently use to conduct recognition tests make us question their value. Before they perform a test, they make arrangements for the child to meet the previous family. Often, when word spreads that a child claiming to remember the life of a particular previous personality is coming to meet the family members of that person, a large crowd gathers before the child arrives. Someone then either asks the child, for example, "Do you see your wife?" or gives him a small item to take to the individual in question. As Dr. Stevenson has written, though those involved are not automatically assuming that the child is remembering the life of a particular individual and are trying to test the child, the crowd of people assembled to watch the testing may look expectantly at the wife of the previous personality when someone asks the child to identify her, and an observant child can hardly fail to point out the right person.

These apparent recognitions frequently impress those involved in the case. Though their hopes that the child will recognize the individuals from the previous life may well cloud their judgment, we should note in fairness that the manner of the child during the recognition—for instance, a look of recognition or of warm emotion—may make the event more impressive for those who experienced it. Witnesses do not always say that the child recognized the previous family members, or they may report that the child was able to recognize some but not all of the family members.

In some cases, informants have reported that the child recognized individuals from the previous life when few if any people were there who could have inadvertently identified the family members. This can occur if the previous family learns of the child's statements before the child's family has gone to verify them and goes unannounced to see the child at his home. Indika Ishwara in Chapter 4 told his mother, "Father has come," when the father of the previous personality visited his family.

In other situations, the families conduct additional tests requiring the child to have knowledge of the previous life in order to answer correctly. For instance, in the case of Chanai Choomalaiwong in Chapter 4, the previous family showed him five or six gunbelts and asked him to pick out his. He immediately picked the one that belonged to the previous personality. Just as with the uncontrolled recognition tests for family members, we do not know if family members unintentionally guided him in selecting the correct one.

In some cases, the parents of subjects have reported that the children led the way to the home of the previous personality. This occurred in Chanai's case, when he described the life of a schoolteacher and then led the way to the home of the parents of a murdered schoolteacher. In that instance, and in a number of others like it, no one who knew the way was with the child, so we do not have to consider the possibility that the child picked up unintentional cues from those nearby.

Some children also seem to recognize changes that have taken place since the death of the previous personality. For instance, when Sujith Jayaratne from Chapter 5 was taken to the property of the parents of the previous personality, Sammy Fernando, he commented correctly that the road had been moved and that some of the fencing was new since Sammy had died. In addition, he went to a place where a tree had been removed after Sammy's death and asked, "Where is the tree that was here?"

Similarly, Gamini Jayasena in Chapter 5 went to the home of the previous personality, Palitha Senewiratne. After Palitha's death, his family had replaced a thatched roof with one of corrugated iron, and Gamini commented to Palitha's parents that the roof had not been "shiny" in the past the way that it was then. When he visited the boardinghouse where Palitha had stayed while attending school, he told the owner that an olive tree had previously been there, and in fact one had been cut down after Palitha's death.

In other cases, families may have conducted recognition tests under conditions that we would not judge to be adequate, but the children have then made impressive statements afterwards. After identifying the widow of the previous personality, Necip Ünlütaşkiran in Chapter 4 said that he had cut her on the leg with a knife, and she confirmed that her husband had indeed done so during an argument.

In another example, when Jasbir Singh, the boy in Chapter 6 who refused to eat non-Brahmin food, saw a cousin of the previous personality, he said, "Come in, Gandhiji." Someone corrected him by saying, "This is Birbal," and Jasbir responded, "We call him Gandhiji." In fact, the man did have the nickname of Gandhiji, because people thought that his large ears made him look like Mahatma Gandhi.

These spontaneous observations undermine the idea that the subjects' parents have coached them to pretend to remember the previous lives. The knowledge the children have shown involved information that the parents would not have, and the children have demonstrated an ability to do more than recite facts about the previous life.

Some children also make spontaneous recognitions in which

they happen to recognize a person or place even though no one was intending to conduct a recognition test. In such circumstances, the environmental cues that may help the children succeed in the uncontrolled tests are generally not present. At times, they lead to a case being solved when otherwise it likely would not have been. An example of this is Gamini Jayasena in Chapter 5, who commented on a bus trip that his previous home had been at a particular stop, and this led his family to investigate the people in that area. Likewise, in Necip Ünlütaşkiran's case, his parents did not attempt to verify his statements about a past life until he met his grandfather's wife. At that point, he said that he recognized her from the past life that he had described being in a location, the city of Mersin, where she had previously lived. Similarly, Ratana Wongsombat in Chapter 5 recognized the nun Mae Chan, so her father went back to her temple to talk with her. He then learned that his daughter's statements about a past life were accurate for a woman who had died one and a half years before Ratana was born. In that case, Ratana had asked to go to the temple, so her recognition was not the coincidence that Gamini's appears to be.

The Case of Nazih Al-Danaf

One case that involved several recognitions is the case of Nazih Al-Danaf in Lebanon. At a very early age, Nazih described a past life to his parents and his seven siblings, all of whom were available for interviews. Nazih described the life of a man that his family did not know. He said that the man carried pistols and grenades, that he had a pretty wife and young children, that he had a two-story house with trees around it and a cave nearby, that he had a mute friend, and that he had been shot by a group of men.

His father reported that Nazih demanded that his parents take him to his previous house in a small town ten miles away. They took him to that town, along with two of his sisters and a brother, when he was six years old. About a half mile from the town, Nazih asked them to stop at a dirt road running off the main road. He told them that the road came to a dead end where there was a cave, but they drove on without confirming this. When they got to the center of town, six roads converged, and Nazih's father asked him which way to go. Nazih pointed to one of the roads and said to go on it until they came to a road that forked off upward, where they would see his house. When they got to the first fork that went up, the family got out and began asking about anyone who had died in the way that Nazih had described.

They quickly discovered that a man named Fuad, who had a house on that road before dying ten years prior to Nazih's birth, seemed to fit Nazih's statements. Fuad's widow asked Nazih, "Who built the foundation of this gate at the entrance of the house?" and Nazih correctly answered, "A man from the Faraj family." The group then went into the house, where Nazih correctly described how Fuad had kept his weapons in a cupboard. The widow asked him if she had had an accident at their previous home, and Nazih gave accurate details of her accident. She also asked if he remembered what had made their young daughter seriously ill, and Nazih correctly responded that she had accidentally taken some of her father's pills. He also accurately described a couple of other incidents from the previous personality's life.

The widow and her five children were all very impressed with the knowledge that Nazih demonstrated, and they were all convinced that he was the rebirth of Fuad.

Soon after that meeting, Nazih visited Fuad's brother, Sheikh Adeeb. When Nazih saw him, he ran up saying, "Here comes my brother Adeeb." Sheikh Adeeb asked Nazih for proof that he was his brother, and Nazih said, "I gave you a Checki 16." A Checki 16 is a type of pistol from Czechoslovakia that is not common in Lebanon, and Fuad had indeed given his brother one. Sheikh Adeeb then asked Nazih where his original house was, and Nazih led him down the road until he said correctly, "This is the house of my father and this [the next house] is my first house." They went in the latter house, where Fuad's first wife still lived, and when Sheikh Adeeb later asked who she was, Nazih correctly gave her name.

Sheikh Adeeb then showed Nazih a photograph of three men and asked him who they were. Nazih pointed to each and correctly gave the names of Adeeb, Fuad, and a deceased brother of theirs. Sheikh Adeeb showed Nazih another picture, and Nazih said correctly that the man in it was the father of those men. Later, Sheikh Adeeb visited Nazih's home, and he took a handgun with him. He asked Nazih if this was the gun that Fuad had given him, and Nazih correctly said that it was not.

Dr. Haraldsson investigated Nazih's case, and he was able to verify most of the statements that Nazih made, including the claim that the previous personality had a mute friend. He also found out that Nazih's description of Fuad's house matched another one in which Fuad lived for several years, including the time during which the house in town, which was not fully completed at the time of Fuad's death, was being built. The former house was by the dirt road that Nazih had pointed out during the family's first visit to the previous town, and a cave was also at the end of it as Nazih had said.

If the families in this case are remembering events correctly, then Nazih's statements are very difficult to explain by normal means. His spontaneous recognitions of the locations of two houses that the previous personality had owned are quite impressive by themselves. Adding his ability to correctly point out the previous personality's first house makes coincidence seem an unlikely explanation. On top of these, his statements to Fuad's family about various small details are also notable. His statement about the Checki 16 pistol is particularly impressive in a number of ways, one being that this knowledge could not have arisen from any environmental cues. His ability to state the names of the men in a picture is more impressive than cases in which a child simply points to a member of the previous personality's family, since environmental cues would not lead him to know the names that he gave. The informants stated that Nazih had not seen pictures of the previous personality before he identified him in the group photograph, and Sheikh Adeeb was certain that with the possible exception of his wife, no one knew that Fuad had given him a Checki 16 pistol.

In a limited number of cases, investigators have been able to conduct controlled recognition tests in which the child appeared able to recognize individuals from the life of the previous personality. Such tests occurred in the following two cases that Dr. Stevenson investigated.

The Case of Gnanatilleka Baddewithana

Gnanatilleka Baddewithana was born in Sri Lanka in 1956, and when she was two years old, she began saying that she had a mother and father along with two brothers and many sisters in another place. After hearing about a town, Talawakelle, that was sixteen miles away, Gnanatilleka began saying that she had lived there, and she said that she wanted to visit her former parents there.

When Gnanatilleka was four and a half years old, a neighbor wrote about her to H.S.S. Nissanka, a journalist who had written several articles about reincarnation and who later obtained a Ph.D. in International Relations. He subsequently wrote a book about Gnanatilleka's case, and I have taken numerous details from it. Dr. Nissanka decided to go see the girl, and he asked a well-known Buddhist monk and a teacher at a nearby college to accompany him. They interviewed Gnanatilleka, and she described a number of incidents from a life in Talawakelle, including one in which she saw the Queen as she traveled by train.

She had not given any names other than Talawakelle and a sister named Lora—or sometimes Dora. Since Queen Elizabeth had traveled through Sri Lanka in 1954, Dr. Nissanka and his companions assumed that Gnanatilleka was describing someone from Talawakelle who had died between the time of that visit and Gnanatilleka's birth in 1956. Actually, they assumed that the previous personality must have died before Gnanatilleka's conception, but that is not an assumption that we would automatically share. Dr. Nissanka wrote two articles about the case for a popular weekly newspaper, and the three men then went to Talawakelle to investigate.

While in Talawakelle, the group met a man who said that the information in the articles matched the life of a family member, a teenage boy named Tillekeratne, who had died in November of 1954. Soon after that meeting, Tillekeratne's teacher went to Gnanatilleka's home along with two men that Tillekeratne had not known. Each of the men asked Gnanatilleka if she knew him. She said no to two of them, but to her teacher, she said, "Yes, you are from Talawakelle!" After a moment, she commented that he had taught her and had never punished her, and she climbed into his lap.

The next day, the investigation team arranged for Gnanatilleka to meet members of Tillekeratne's family at a rest house, or inn, in Talawakelle, but they did not tell Gnanatilleka the reason for her trip there. Gnanatilleka sat in a room with her mother, the monk, and Dr. Nissanka, who recorded the events with a tape recorder. Gnanatilleka's father and Tillekeratne's teacher stood near the door, and other observers watched from the next room. Tillekeratne's mother then entered the room. The monk asked Gnanatilleka, "Do you know her?"

Gnanatilleka looked up and suddenly appeared excited, and she stared at the woman. When asked again if she knew her, Gnanatilleka said, "Yes."

Tillekeratne's mother handed her a candy bar and then held her arms out to Gnanatilleka, who quickly hugged her. Tillekeratne's mother said, "Tell me, where did I live?"

Gnanatilleka slowly answered, "Talawakelle."

Tillekeratne's mother said, "So tell me who I am."

Gnanatilleka, after making sure that her own mother could not hear her, whispered to Tillekeratne's mother (and to Dr. Nissanka's microphone), "Talawakelle mother."

After a minute, the observers asked Gnanatilleka again, "Who was that lady . . . tell us," and she replied, "She's my Talawakelle mother."

Next, Tillekeratne's father came in, and Gnanatilleka was asked, "Do you know him?"

She answered yes, and when she was asked who he was, she answered, "He's my Talawakelle father."

Following him, one of Tillekeratne's sisters, one who had accompanied him to school every day, came in, and when Gnanatilleka was asked who she was, she replied, "This is my sister from Talawakelle."

"Where did you go with this sister?"

"To school."

When asked how they had gone, she correctly answered that they had gone by train.

Coming in next was a man who had moved to Talawakelle after Tillekeratne died. He asked her, "Who am I?"

"No."

Dr. Nissanka asked her, "Do you know him? Look again carefully, who is he?"

She answered, "No, I don't know him."

Three women came in next. One asked, "Do you know me? Who am I?"

Gnanatilleka answered, "Yes, you're my fair sister."

Another asked, "Who am I?"

"The sister who lives in the house below ours."

Gnanatilleka's mother then asked her who the third woman was, and she answered, "The sister to whose house we go to sew clothes." These were all correct for Tillekeratne's sisters.

Two men from Talawakelle were sent in separately. One was a very close friend of Tillekeratne's family, while the other one had taught Tillekeratne at Sunday School. Gnanatilleka said that she knew each of them at Talawakelle but did not give other specifics.

Lastly, Tillekeratne's brother went in. He and Tillekeratne had constantly quarreled, and when Gnanatilleka was asked if she knew him, she angrily answered, "No!" She was asked again, and she answered, "No! No!" Dr. Nissanka then told her that she could tell just her mother if she knew him, so she whispered to her mother, "My brother from Talawakelle." Dr. Nissanka asked her to let everyone else hear, so she said, "My brother from Talawakelle." When Dr. Nissanka told Gnanatilleka to let the brother hold her, she began crying and said that she would not.

Gnanatilleka made some very impressive recognitions, as she not only knew the relationship that the previous personality had with each individual but other facts that she could not have known from appearance alone. She stated correctly that she had not known individuals that the previous personality had not known—the two men who accompanied Tillekeratne's teacher to her home and the stranger whom the investigators brought in as a test for her.

Gnanatilleka also made a couple of spontaneous recognitions later. She developed a relationship with Tillekeratne's teacher, and one day when they were out together, Gnanatilleka pointed to a woman in a crowd of people and said, "I know her." She told the teacher, "She came to the Talawakelle temple with me," and he confirmed with the woman that she had been friendly with Tillekeratne when they worshipped at the temple. Another time, Gnanatilleka pointed out one woman who was in a group of others and said, "She is angry with my Talawakelle mother." The teacher checked with the woman and found out that she was a neighbor of Tillekeratne's family who had previously had disagreements with Tillekeratne's mother, but they had since patched up their differences.

Dr. Stevenson arrived on the scene a year after the controlled recognition tests and interviewed people from both families as well as Tillekeratne's teacher. Following the initial interviews, he continued to check on the family from time to time. One item that he discovered was that Tillekeratne did not have a sister named Lora or Dora. He had been classmates with a girl named Lora when he was younger, and they had had some contact before his death. Dr. Stevenson interviewed her in 1970. She had never met Gnanatilleka, so he took her and one of her friends, whom Tillekeratne had not known, unannounced to Gnanatilleka's home. He asked Gnanatilleka, who was almost fifteen years old by that time, if she could recognize the two women. She called Lora "Dora," confusing the names just as she had done as a young child, and said that she had known her in Talawakelle, but she could give no other details.

This was a remarkable accomplishment, even if we accept the possibility of reincarnation, since Lora had gone from being a teenager during Tillekeratne's life to being an approximately thirty-year-old woman, though we might suppose that this was not so different from being able to recognize an old classmate at a high school reunion. Gnanatilleka did accomplish the recognition. Though she might have guessed the location of Talawakelle, given the context of Dr. Stevenson's previous contact with the family, her ability to state the name, which she had not given for any of the other women that people had asked her to identify, demonstrated knowledge that is hard to dismiss.

Gnanatilleka's case was a sex-change case, but she did not show particularly masculine traits. When she was young, her parents noted that she was more boyish than her sister was, but not to a severe degree, and as a teenager, her appearance was that of a typical Sinhalese girl. The previous personality, however, tended to be rather feminine. He preferred to be with girls and at times painted his fingernails. He enjoyed sewing and liked silk shirts. In that area at that time, these characteristics made him different from most of the other boys.

The Case of Ma Choe Hnin Htet

The case of Ma Choe Hnin Htet in Myanmar involved not only a controlled recognition test but also an experimental birthmark. The previous personality in the case was a young woman, Ma Lai Lai Way, who was born with a heart defect. It limited her functioning significantly, and she was still attending high school at the age of twenty when she entered the Rangoon General Hospital for several months in 1975. She underwent open-heart surgery there and died during the surgery.

Following Ma Lai Lai Way's death, three of her friends offered to prepare her body for cremation. As they were doing this, they recalled the custom of marking a body, so they used red lipstick to make a mark on the left side of the back of her neck. They chose this spot as opposed to more visible ones, because they did not want a future child to be disfigured. Dr. Stevenson has pointed out that in choosing the back of the neck, the girls picked the worst possible site for producing an impressive experimental birthmark since "stork bite" birthmarks are quite common and occasionally persist into later childhood.

Thirteen months after Ma Lai Lai Way's death, her older sister gave birth to a baby girl she named Ma Choe Hnin Htet. After the birth, Ma Choe Hnin Htet's family noted that she had a red birthmark on the left side of the back of her neck. At the time, her family did not know that Ma Lai Lai Way's friends had marked her body, but they learned a few days later when a neighbor told them. Since Ma Choe Hnin Htet's mother did not learn about the body being marked until after she gave birth, we can be sure that maternal impression, the idea that the mother's wishes or expectations could have led to the birthmark on her baby, played no part in this case.

We can also be sure that the position of the birthmark did not lead witnesses to match it incorrectly with the site of the marking, because when Dr. Stevenson talked with one of the friends who had marked the body, Ma Myint Myint Oo, she gave the location without knowing that Ma Choe Hnin Htet had been born with a birthmark. He also interviewed the other two friends, who gave the same location for the marking.

Ma Choe Hnin Htet also had a mark on her chest that presumably was a birthmark, but her family did not notice it for several years, until someone suggested that she might have a birthmark to match Ma Lai Lai Way's surgical incision. It was a thin, pale line, lighter than the rest of her skin, and it ran down the middle of her lower chest and upper abdomen. It matched an incision scar for open-heart surgery, except that it was lower, at least by the time that Ma Choe Hnin Htet was four years old, than an incision for such a surgery would be.

Soon after Ma Choe Hnin Htet became old enough to talk, she spoke of the previous life with her grandparents, the previous personality's parents. She said that her grandmother had been her mother, and she talked of dying when the doctors operated on her. She also said that her name was Lai Lai, and she would cry if family members teased her by telling her that she was not Lai Lai. In addition, she called her mother the term for "older sister," her maternal uncle "brother," and her grandfather "papa."

Dr. Stevenson investigated the case when Ma Choe Hnin Htet was four years old. Three days before his interviews, two of Ma Lai Lai Way's friends, one of whom had marked her body, visited the family. The marker had not seen Ma Choe Hnin Htet since she was a baby, but Ma Choe Hnin Htet was very friendly with her. She walked out to the gate when she saw the women, rather than notifying the adults as she would normally do, and when she met them, she asked the woman to call her Lai Lai Way. She led her to meet her grandmother, who asked her, "Do you know her?" To which Ma Choe Hnin Htet responded, "Yes, of course. We were friends."

When Dr. Stevenson conducted his interviews, he discovered that Ma Myint Myint Oo, another of the women who had marked the body, had never met Ma Choe Hnin Htet. He and his interpreter, U Win Maung, decided to take her to Ma Choe Hnin Htet's home without letting the family know that they were coming. After they arrived at the house, they pointed to Ma Myint Myint Oo and asked Ma Choe Hnin Htet, "Who is she?" Ma Choe Hnin Htet quickly answered, "Myint Myint Oo."

We wish that we had more opportunities to conduct such tests. Unfortunately, the children in our cases have usually met the important figures in the life of the previous personality by the time that we arrive on the scene. During these meetings, the families have frequently judged them to recognize a number of persons from that life, but we have not been able to assess that for ourselves. In order to conduct more tests ourselves, we need to get to the cases sooner. Ideally, getting to a case before anyone has identified the previous personality would give us a wonderful opportunity to arrange such tests, but many such cases may never come to our attention. Some parents may not want others to know that their child is talking about a past life if the case is unsolved and the statements unverified. Even if the parents do not mind others knowing, people are naturally less likely to talk about a case that is unsolved, so our agents in the various countries are less likely to hear of them.

Along these lines, we need to hear about cases early enough so that the children still have the memories. Since most of the children seem to lose the memories by the time they are seven or eight years old, conducting a test when they are older may be fruitless. Exceptions certainly exist, as Dr. Stevenson's test of Gnanatilleka Baddewithana makes clear, but in general, conducting the test while the child is still young is essential. This means that we must hear about cases as early as possible in the subject's life. Unfortunately, our resources are limited, and we often have only one person looking for cases in a given country. If that person learns of a case from a newspaper report, the family has almost always solved it already. Learning of one through other connections offers a better chance of getting to a solvable case before the child has met the previous family, but significant obstacles can remain.

This leaves us with a handful of cases in which investigators have performed adequately controlled recognition tests. This limited number does not mean that these subjects are the only ones to have recognized members of the previous family, but since the conditions under which the other children made the recognitions were not adequately controlled, we cannot say with certainty that they actually did recognize family members.

We would expect that if the children are having real memories of previous lives, they should be able to recognize the people with whom they have described sharing a life, but the memories often seem to be murky and incomplete and only available at certain times for some of the children. If the previous personality has died some time ago, then the appearance of the individuals involved may also have changed substantially from when the previous personality lived. Both of these factors may explain why some of the children fail to recognize members of the previous family.

On the other hand, if we do not accept reincarnation as a possibility, we should be very surprised when a child does recognize individuals from the previous life under controlled conditions. In some ways, these few cases with controlled recognition tests confirm the results of the uncontrolled tests of many other cases, and they constitute an important type of evidence. Any explanation that seeks to dismiss the cases as the result of a normal, mundane process has to deal with these examples of children showing an ability to recognize people from the previous life and to give specific information about them.

Sam, the boy at the beginning of the chapter, appeared to recognize the previous personality, his grandfather, in pictures. When I first heard about those recognitions, I wondered if he could have picked out the previous personality in the class picture because he had just seen the pictures of his grandfather as an older person. When I looked at the pictures, I realized that I could not have picked the previous personality out in the class picture after seeing the others. Thinking a four-year-old child could do so is assuming a lot. In fact, many of the boys in the picture look similar—dark-haired boys wearing the same style clothes—but whether they look similar or not, we should keep in mind that we are talking about a four-year-old boy who picked his grandfather out of the picture. We need to include such recognitions in any overall assessment of this phenomenon. They show that some children not only claim memories of past lives but also seem to show the ability to recognize people or places from those lives.

Considering the Explanations

In trying to explain the recognitions using a normal process, we can easily dismiss the uncontrolled ones as having little scientific value because the children may be able to use environmental cues to figure out who they are being asked to recognize. The statements that the children frequently make during the meetings, such as a person's nickname or details of an event from the past, are more difficult to explain. For these, we must blame faulty memory by the informants about the statements.

We again have to rely on faulty memory by informants to

explain many of the spontaneous recognitions, since the children are said to make statements about the people that show knowledge they seemingly could not have acquired through normal means.

Finally, the controlled recognition tests offer the biggest challenge to explain by a normal process. In the case of Gnanatilleka Baddewithana, she recognized family members of the previous family as researchers brought them in one by one. We might suppose that Gnanatilleka guessed the relationship that each person had with the previous personality, except that she also correctly stated that she did not know a man who the previous personality had not known. In addition, we are giving a four-and-a-half-year-old child a lot of credit to think that her deductive abilities were good enough to enable her to guess all of the relationships correctly.

More problematic still is the fact that she also gave information about the previous personality's sisters that she could not have known from just their appearances. This, along with the recognitions, means that coincidence is not a reasonable explanation, and in addition, we cannot blame faulty memory as an explanation since the researchers made audio recordings of the tests. Fraud seems to be the only possible normal explanation left. We can suppose that Gnanatilleka's family tricked everyone else involved, that the two families conspired to fool the researchers, or that the researchers themselves did not accurately report the events that took place. None of these is likely, especially when we remember that Gnanatilleka was successful in recognizing the woman named Lora when Dr. Stevenson tested her eight years later.

Similarly, Ma Choe Hnin Htet was able to give the name of

one of the previous personality's friends, one who had marked the body, the first time that she met her. Since environmental cues could not have allowed her to know the name, we must suppose that family members lied to Dr. Stevenson when they told him that the girl had never heard the woman's name.

In the cases of controlled recognition tests, fraud is the only normal explanation that we can come up with, and it is not very reasonable. As for the paranormal explanations, any of the three can be used to explain the recognitions. Extrasensory perception could allow the children to be able to identify the previous individuals. If the previous consciousness has possessed the child, it could identify them. Lastly, if the child is the rebirth of the previous personality, then he or she could identify them as well.

CHAPTER 8

Divine Intermission

Bobby Hodges, a boy from North Carolina, frequently talked about wanting to live with his cousins. His cousins' family consisted of one boy, the oldest child, and three girls. In addition, Bobby's aunt had miscarried a set of twins after her son was born. Bobby said that the boy was his big brother and asked why his mother was keeping him from his real family. He repeatedly said that he belonged with his cousins. His parents, thinking that he liked his cousins' family because it had more children in it than his own, never gave his statements much thought until he began talking to his mother one night after his bath when he was four and a half years old.

He asked her if she remembered when he was in her tummy. She said yes and asked if he remembered when his two-and-a-half-year-old brother Donald was in her tummy. He then asked if she remembered when he and Donald were in her tummy at the same time. When she told him that they had not been in her tummy at the same time, he said they were in her tummy at the same time but did not get born. She told him that he did get born and later Donald was born. He responded that he and Donald had been in his Aunt Susan's tummy at the same time, rather than his mother's, and asked why Aunt Susan did not give birth to them.

Bobby then became very upset and began screaming at Donald. He said, "Donald, it is all your fault. I told you I wanted to get born real bad, and you didn't want to. How did you take me out of there, Donald? Why didn't you want to get born? Tell me how you did it. Tell me how you took me out of there."

At this point, Bobby's mother had to restrain him to keep him from going after Donald. She told him not to scream at Donald and that Donald did not know what he was talking about. Bobby screamed that Donald did know and asked him again why he had taken Bobby out of Aunt Susan's tummy.

Donald then took his pacifier out of his mouth and yelled, "No! I wanted Daddy!" before popping his pacifier back in. Bobby yelled back, "I didn't want Daddy, I wanted Uncle Ron!"

After Bobby calmed down somewhat, he told his mother that after the failed pregnancy, he had tried to get back in Aunt Susan's tummy, but Rebecca, his cousin, was there. He told his mother, "I wanted to be in there, and she wouldn't let me. I tried to kick her out, but it didn't work. She got to be born, and I didn't." He said that he then got in his mother's tummy and was born. He said, "I sure did have to work hard to get here, Mom."

To give some background, Bobby's Uncle Ron is his father's brother. Ron's wife Susan became pregnant with male twins seven years before Bobby was born. At thirty-three weeks' gestation, Susan did not feel any movement from the twins, and when she went to the hospital, the doctors found that both had died. The hospital records indicate that the attachment of one of the umbilical cords to the placenta did not have adequate coverings around the blood vessels and so was very susceptible to being compressed. The doctors told Susan that they suspected that one of the twins rolled over on the cord there. This stopped the blood flow, killing one twin, and because of shared circulation, the other one died soon thereafter.

Since the miscarriages were understandably upsetting to the parents, the family never spoke of them, and Bobby's parents feel sure that he had never heard about them. Susan and Ron became pregnant again a few months later, and they subsequently had three girls. The last one, Rebecca, was born eighteen months before Bobby was.

In addition to his talk of being one of Susan's twins, Bobby made a few comments about other lives that he said he remembered. He said that in one, he died from a gunshot wound, and in another, he was a teenager who died in a motor vehicle accident. One time, after recovering from the flu, Bobby told his mother, "Mom, people in the other world don't get sick." She responded, "The other world, Bobby?" and he said, "The world where I was waiting to get born. People don't get sick there. They are just happy and never get sick. I wish we didn't get sick in this world."

Another time, he talked about his parents' wedding, which occurred when his mother was pregnant with him. Since she was noticeably pregnant at the ceremony, she does not have any wedding pictures on display in their house. She and her husband got married in a gazebo on a hill, and they had to climb steps up to the hill and again into the gazebo. They do not believe that Bobby had ever seen a picture of the wedding or heard them discuss it, until one day Bobby saw his mother looking through a pile of pictures. She gave him a picture of his parents' wedding—a close-up shot of them standing in front of a railing. It is the railing of the gazebo, but that is not obvious from the picture. His mother is holding flowers, and his father is wearing a boutonniere. They are standing in profile, apparently facing the minister, but the back of a woman, presumably a member of the wedding party, blocks the viewer from seeing the person in front of them.

When Bobby's mother asked him if he knew what it was a picture of, he answered, "Yes, Mom. It's a picture of you and Dad getting married. I was there. I saw the whole thing." She asked, "You did?" and he answered, "Yes, Mom, you walked up the stairs, and then you gave each other rings, and then you ate cake."

I happened to call her immediately after this exchange, and she told me what Bobby had said. She did not see any way he could have known that she and her husband walked up stairs to start their wedding. At the one wedding he had attended, cake had not been served because of an air-conditioning problem. His mother does not normally even eat cake, but she did so at her own wedding, because she thought that not eating it might bring bad luck.

On his fourth birthday, Bobby had talked about being born. His mother reports that he was born by cesarean section after a prolonged labor. He had presented in a face-up position, called an occiput-posterior position, and nurses were unable to get him to turn. When Bobby talked about his birth, he said that he had been kicking in the womb because he was trying to get out. His mother responded that he had to wait to get born, and he said, "I know, and it was making me mad, and I was pushing to get out and then they were pushing on my head, Mom, trying to get me to go back in, and that was making me really mad, 'cause I wanted to get out, but I couldn't 'cause I was stuck."

His mother was shocked and said, "Yes, you were stuck, and they were pushing on your head to get you to turn over. All you had to do was turn over, and you could have gotten out."

He responded, "Oh, I didn't know that. I would have turned over, but I thought they were pushing me back in. Anyway, then I saw the light, and then the doctor took me out of your tummy, and then they cleaned all that slime off, and then they put me in a bed, and then I could get some sleep."

Bobby's case is an example of one in which the child talks about the interval between the death of the previous personality and his birth. In his case, he talked about events that took place when he was in his mother's womb and made one reference to being in another world before coming to his mother. Most of the subjects in our cases do not make such statements. In 1,100 cases, sixty-nine subjects reported memories of the previous personality's funeral or the handling of the remains; ninety-one described other events happening on Earth; 112 reported memories of being in another realm; and forty-five reported memories either of conception or of being reborn. Some of the children are counted in more than one category since they described more than one type of experience, and only 217 out of the 1,100 reported having at least one of these experiences.

Since we obviously cannot verify any claims that the children make about another realm and often cannot verify the other statements about experiences between lives, the intermission memories tend to be a more speculative area than the other parts of the cases. A couple of factors suggest that we should at least consider the statements. First, some children have made statements about events that occurred that were later verified as accurate. Limited evidence exists in those cases that supports the children's claims to remember events that took place between lives, and we will briefly look at several of those shortly.

Children in the stronger cases tend to make these statements more often than children do in the weaker ones, adding some support for their validity. I developed a scale that rates the strength of each case. When we look at the different types of intermission memories—ones of the previous personality's funeral, ones of other events, ones of being in another realm, and ones of conception or birth—either individually or as a group, we find that the likelihood that a child will report them has a positive correlation with the score that the child gets on the strength-of-case scale. Poonam Sharma, a medical student working with us, also ran statistics that showed that the children who report intermission memories are more likely to remember the name of the previous personality and the way that the person died than are the children who do not report them. They tend to remember more names from the previous life in general, and they make more statements about that life that are later verified to be accurate.

A number of the reports are fascinating in any event and seem worth noting.

Hanging Around

Twenty-five out of 1,100 subjects described details of the previous personality's funeral or the handling of the remains that were verified to be accurate. One example is Ratana Wongsombat from Chapter 5, who correctly described the previous personality's ashes being spread under the bo tree of the temple complex rather than being buried as she had wanted. Sometimes, the statements are not specific enough to be verifiable. For instance, Purnima Ekanayake from Chapter 4 said that after her fatal accident, she floated in the air in semi-darkness for several days. She saw people crying for her and saw her body at the funeral. She said that many people were floating around as she was. She then saw some light, went to it, and came to her new family.

The children who make comments about the funeral of the previous personality do not tend to make many of them, so they do not seem to focus on it. If we accept the statements that they do make, they imply that the consciousness of the previous personality stayed around the body or the family for a while after the death.

Some children have reported that they stayed for an extended amount of time after the funeral. In some instances, the previous family has confirmed some of the statements. A boy in India named Veer Singh claimed to remember the life of Som Dutt, a boy from a village five miles away who died eleven years before Veer Singh was born. He said that he stayed around Som Dutt's home and lived in a tree. He said that he went to the wedding of Som Dutt's brother during that time and gave details about the type of food served. Though he was correct, the food was typical for an Indian wedding. He also said that he went with family members when they left the house. This memory matched a dream that Som Dutt's mother had several months after Som Dutt's death in which he came to her and said that he was going with his brother as he sneaked out of the house at night to attend fairs. After the dream, the brother admitted to his mother that he had been leaving the house. Veer Singh also reported that he had become irritated by some women playing on a swing suspended from the tree where he was staying and had broken the plank of the swing. Som Dutt's father remembered that such an accident had taken place. Veer Singh talked with Som Dutt's mother about lawsuits that the family had become involved in after Som Dutt's death. He talked of siblings who had been born during the intermission, and he correctly told Som Dutt's father that a particular man had moved from the village after Som Dutt's death.

Other children talk of staying near the area where they died in the previous life. A good example of this is Bongkuch Promsin, a boy in Thailand who appeared to remember the life of an eighteen-year-old man who was murdered eight years before Bongkuch's birth in a town six miles from his village. He made twenty-nine statements about the previous life that were verified to be accurate, including descriptions of the actions of the killers immediately after they murdered the previous personality. He said that he stayed for seven years over a bamboo tree near where they left the previous personality's body. After seven years, he went to look for the previous personality's mother on a rainy day. He said that he got lost in the market, saw his future father, and decided to go with him on the bus to his future home. In fact, Bongkuch's father had attended a meeting in that area on a rainy day during the month when Bongkuch was conceived, so Bongkuch's memories were at least partially verified.

Reports of Another Realm

Subjects in other cases have described experiences in another realm during the interval between death and rebirth. A boy named Lee said that he remembered deciding to be reborn. He said that other beings helped him with his decision to come down to Earth. He also said that his previous mother was prettier than his current one, who accepted the comparison with good humor. William, the boy in Chapter 1, said that he floated up after dying, and he talked about being in heaven, where he saw God as well as animals.

Sam Taylor, the boy in Chapter 7 who picked his grandfather out of a grammar school class picture, also talked of seeing God. He said that God gave him a card to come back from heaven, and as he described it, it looked like a business card with green arrows on it. Along with this rather fanciful-sounding detail, he said that his body shot up to heaven when he died and that someone else died at the same time he had. In addition, Sam talked about seeing Uncle Phil in heaven. His grandfather's best friend was the husband of his wife's sister, and the grandfather called him Uncle Phil. Sam commented that in his previous life he had made Uncle Phil's feet hot. His grandfather and Uncle Phil enjoyed playing pranks on each other, and his grandfather would give Phil a "hot foot" by warming his shoes before Phil put them on.

Similarly, Patrick Christenson, the boy in Chapter 4 with three birthmarks that matched lesions on his deceased half-brother, spoke of talking in heaven with a relative named "Billy the Pirate," who he said told him about being shot at close range and dying while up in the mountains. Patrick's mother reported that she had never heard of such a relative, but when she called her mother to ask about Patrick's statements, she learned that a cousin with the nickname Billy the Pirate had in fact died that way.

Other particularly vivid descriptions of another realm include those of Disna Samarasinghe, a girl in Sri Lanka who made numerous statements about the life of an elderly woman who died in a village three miles away. She described being lifted up, even though her body was buried, and flying like a bird. She talked of meeting a king or governor whose reddish clothes and beautiful pointed shoes were never taken off, never dirty, and never washed. The same was true for her own clothes except that they were golden. She said that she played at the king's home, which was made of glass and had beautiful red beds. She said that when she got hungry there, she simply thought of food and it appeared. The sight of the food satisfied her appetite, so she did not need to eat it. She said that the king took her to the home of her new family after asking her to go there.

Another child who made similar statements is Sunita Khandelwal, a girl in India who talked about the life of a woman from a city 220 miles away. She reported that after a fatal fall from a balcony, "I went up. There was a *baba* (holy man) with a long beard. They checked my record and said, 'Send her back.' There are some rooms there. I have seen God's house. It is very nice. You do not know everything that is there."

Certainly, no one would disagree with that last remark.

Memories from Earth Versus Another Realm

One issue for us to consider is why some children describe an existence in this world after the previous death while others describe one in another world. If we take these reports seriously, we can consider what factors might lead an individual to have one type of experience after death compared to the other. Two we can examine are the way that the previous personality died and the suddenness of that death. In looking at the way that the previous personality died, we can compare natural deaths to unnatural ones to see if the two types could produce different types of experiences afterwards. Unnatural deaths include accidents, drownings, and any violent deaths, whether intentional or unintentional. When we compare the two types for 1,100 cases, we find that whether the previous personality died by natural versus unnatural means does not seem to affect whether the child in the case will later talk about earthly events that occurred after the death. On the other hand, cases in which the previous personality died by natural means are slightly but significantly more likely to include statements about an existence in another realm than ones involving unnatural means—19 percent of the natural means cases versus 13 percent of the unnatural means ones.

We can look at the issue of suddenness of death in two ways. First, when we consider how long the death was expected, we divide the cases into five categories—unexpected up until the time of death, up until the day of death, up until the week of death, up until the month of death, or expected for more than one month. When we look to see how that length of time correlates with the subsequent statements that the children make about each kind of experience during the time between lives, we find that the suddenness does not affect how likely the child will be to describe memories about events in this world, but the more unexpected the death, the less likely the subject will be to make statements about an existence in another realm.

The other way to look at the issue of suddenness of death is to compare deaths that were unexpected at the time of death with ones that were expected for at least some length of time, even if it is only part of a day. In other words, we are comparing cases in which the previous personality died instantly with ones in which he or she did not. Instant deaths would include many deaths by unnatural means but would also include deaths by natural means in cases in which the person died immediately from, for instance, a heart attack. When we make the comparison, again we see no difference in the frequency of statements about earthly events. On the other hand, cases in which the previous personality died suddenly are less likely to include statements by the children about an existence in another realm than ones are where the person did not die suddenly—12 percent versus 22 percent.

This analysis suggests that how the previous personality dies or how suddenly he or she dies does not change the likelihood that the child in the case will talk later about earthly events that took place between that death and the child's birth. On the other hand, cases in which the previous personality's death occurred by natural means or was expected are somewhat more likely to include subjects' statements about an existence in another realm between the time of the previous personality's death and the child's birth.

Though we might take from this that dying a violent or unexpected death somehow short-circuits the process and decreases a person's chances of going on to another world, these findings, though statistically significant, are not absolute. We should also realize that if individuals go to another realm when they die and then come back to earth to be reborn, this analysis suggests that the way that a person dies and the suddenness of that death may be two factors that can affect how likely *memories* of the other realm are—but not necessarily how likely the experiences themselves are.

While we are speculating, we can look at whether personality and behavioral characteristics of the previous personality affect the likelihood that the subject of a case will describe earthly events or ones from another realm. The features of the previous personality we register in our computer database include the following: Was PP (the previous personality) attached to wealth? Was PP a criminal? Was PP philanthropic or generous? Was PP active in religious observances? Was PP a meditator? And, was PP saintly? I should add that we do not have information on the items for most of our cases, so we are dealing with small numbers—not so small that we cannot do statistical analyses with them, but small enough that we need to be aware that any interpretations are preliminary.

When we look to see if any of these characteristics affect the chances that the child will later report intermission memories, we find that none of them affect the likelihood of memories of earthly events. In addition, none of them affect the likelihood of memories of another realm except for one—being a meditator. We only have information on whether the previous personality meditated in thirty-three of the 1,100 cases in the database, so these results are preliminary in the extreme, but nonetheless statistically significant. The more that the previous personality meditated, the more likely the child was to describe memories from another realm.

I obtained these results when I used the question of the child recalling an existence in another realm as a yes/no question—either the child recalled an existence or not. We actually do not code the item of recalling an existence in another realm as a yes/no question, but as a question of degree. We rate whether the child recalled an existence in another realm in great detail, in some detail, in little detail, or not at all. When we break the item down this way and compare it to the previous personality's tendency to meditate, we still get a positive correlation. This means that the more the previous personality meditated, the more detail the child subsequently used in describing events in another realm. Given this, if we are open to the possibility of reincarnation and if we are going to draw any conclusion from this at all, then it should be that meditating might increase the ability of individuals to recall an existence in another realm in their next life. This is quite different from saying that meditating might increase an individual's chances of being able to go to another realm after a life, but that is also a possibility. Any conclusion at all is preliminary. Another factor could be involved that creates the illusion of a correlation between meditating and recall of another realm.

I also looked at the other personality characteristics of the previous personality to see if they affect the degree of the child's recall of another realm, and none of them does. Our current, preliminary information indicates that the ability to have memories of earthly events or of another realm after dying is not affected by whether a person was attached to wealth, was a criminal, was philanthropic or generous, was active in religious observances, or was saintly. These statistical tests, of course, only look at the likelihood that the child will report memories, and they do not answer the question of whether any of these factors could influence the likelihood of continuing to exist after dying or of being reincarnated.

Memorable Pregnancies

The last type of intermission memory involves those of conception or of being reborn. This category can also include memories either of the baby's experiences in the womb or of the parents' actions during the pregnancy, as in Bobby's case at the beginning of the chapter. He reported memories of his parents' wedding as well as of his birth. Another example is William from Chapter 1. When he saw a picture of his mother when she was pregnant, he commented that when he was in her tummy, she always held it when she ran up the stairs of their previous house. She asked him how he knew that, and he said that he knew because he had been watching her. As for memories of being born, many scientists have thought that infants were incapable of retaining memories for longer than a few seconds or minutes at most. If that was true, then children's claims to remember their births would clearly be impossible.

Our understanding of infant memory has been undergoing change because of recent research. In the past, conventional wisdom held that infants possessed a primitive memory system, while a different, more mature system developed late in the first year of life. Scientists spoke of implicit or procedural memory in infants and explicit or declarative memory that developed later. This conventional wisdom was not based on solid research. As one researcher has noted, "Most scientists probably believe that there is empirical evidence for the conclusion that different systems mediate the retention of different types of acquired knowledge at different points in development, but there is none."

Designing studies of infants' memory has been challenging since they are not able to communicate, but researchers have used various procedures. In some studies, a ribbon is strung from an infant's ankle to a crib mobile so that the baby learns through training that the mobile moves with kicking. If infants see the same mobile in a subsequent session and remember it, they kick more than if they do not remember it. Other techniques have included deferred imitation, which involves having infants reproduce a behavior that an investigator modeled for them earlier. Such studies have indicated, contrary to previous beliefs, that the same fundamental mechanisms are involved in memory processing in infants as in older individuals. In both groups, memories are forgotten gradually; they are recovered by reminders; and they can be changed by new information that overlaps with the old. Studies have shown that the memories of young infants, particularly when they experience appropriate reminders, last longer and are more specific than previously thought. As one researcher has noted, "The growing consensus from the literature on very early memory development is that from the earliest days of life infants can encode, store, and retrieve a great deal of information about events in the world they experience and that they retain this information over considerable time periods."

Though the evidence is clear that infants are able to remember events over longer periods of time as they grow older, the studies indicate that the neural mechanisms associated with the improvement are probably not ones that involve encoding or storing the information. In other words, the fact that most of us cannot recall memories of birth or early infancy does not seem to be due to infants being unable to lay down the memory tracks in their brains in the first place. Instead, the inability to retain such memories is probably due to brain mechanisms that are involved in *retrieving* the memories.

The question becomes whether some children, perhaps through reminders or some other mechanism, are able to retrieve early memories to which most children do not have access. Researchers have documented occasional examples of unusual memory retrieval in children. For example, a child was able at an age of almost three years old to state correctly that a picture he had last seen in a laboratory at the age of nine months was that of a whale. In another study, researchers interviewed ten children under the age of three, and they were all able to recall at least one event that had occurred more than six months earlier. Although young children do not usually have memories of being born—though we might find that more children than we know have such memories if we were to ask—this research suggests that such a possibility is not the crazy idea that conventional wisdom has held it to be. When Bobby, the boy at the beginning of the chapter, appears to remember events from his birth, we may conclude that he is demonstrating an unusual or even extraordinary ability to retrieve early memories, but that is different from saying that he could not possibly remember them since infants are not able to encode memories in their brains.

Now let us move on to prenatal memories—ones of events that occur when a baby is developing in the womb. In one study, researchers asked pregnant women to read a passage from a children's story aloud every day for the last six weeks of their pregnancy. Two days after the babies were born, testing was done in which a recording of that passage was played to reward one pattern of sucking while a recording of a different passage was played to reward another pattern of sucking. The results demonstrated that the babies preferred hearing the original passage compared to the new one. When babies whose mothers had not read the passage were tested, they showed no preference. The study indicated that the babies could retain memories that were created before they were born for at least two days after birth.

Reports like Bobby's involve much more than showing a

preference for one story over another. What about more involved memories? Dr. David Cheek, an obstetrician, elicited fetal memories from subjects through hypnosis and ideomotor techniques, in which he taught hypnotized subjects to answer questions using finger signals that were out of their conscious control. As I will discuss in Chapter 10, hypnosis can be an unreliable tool for obtaining accurate memories, but Dr. Cheek got some accurate ones with the process. In one report, he described four cases in which hypnotized subjects reported memories from the womb that their mothers later verified were accurate. In the first case, a girl remembered a scene in which her father became upset when he saw that her mother, while pregnant, was knitting an item for a girl. The subject remembered her mother saying, "It has to be a girl!" along with the fact that she was wearing a dark green plaid dress. Her mother confirmed the details and added that she had given away the dress soon after her pregnancy, meaning that the girl could not have seen it later.

In another case, Dr. Cheek treated a woman in the early 1960s who remembered an incident under hypnosis that occurred when her mother was six months pregnant with her. Her mother began to attempt an abortion with a buttonhook after her husband, who was an alcoholic, threatened to kill her. The mother could not go through with the act, and she never spoke to the subject about it until after the daughter recalled it under hypnosis.

In the next case, a man recalled an incident in which his mother, while pregnant with him, learned that his grandfather had died suddenly of a heart attack, accurately describing the dress that his mother was wearing. He also described his mother's fear during labor that she would die as her father recently had.

His mother later confirmed his memories of her appearance as well as of her emotions.

In the last case, a German woman remembered that her mother felt scared when she learned that she was pregnant, as her father was in combat in World War II at the time. The woman also recalled that when she was born, the doctor told her mother in a flat voice, "The baby is very beautiful" while her mother was very happy. Her mother confirmed that these memories were accurate. Though the delivery room greeting seems somewhat distinctive, we may wonder if the woman could have deduced that her mother would have been initially anxious about the pregnancy given the events going on then.

Dr. Cheek thought that the subjects initially stored the memories as sensory impressions while in the womb and then organized them later after being capable of understanding language, much as a person might tape a lecture in a foreign language and then listen to it years later after learning the language. He concluded that the fetus's experience mirrors what the mother perceives and responds to in her environment throughout the pregnancy. The evidence suggested to him that telepathy, clairvoyance, and some form of hearing are available to the fetus once its mother knows that she is pregnant. Though such a conclusion seems premature, I cannot come up with a better explanation for some of the cases that he describes.

His cases differ from ours in that they involve memories that adult subjects are not consciously aware of until their hypnotic sessions, but if we conclude that subjects can access the memories through hypnosis as adults, then the idea that some young children would have conscious awareness of them does not seem so unlikely. Dr. Cheek's reports undermine the idea that infants at birth, or even before birth, are incapable of laying down memory tracks, since his subjects were later able to recall events from those times while they were under hypnosis.

The memories that Dr. Cheek documented are like the ones that some of our subjects claim about birth or their time in the womb, but they differ from memories of another realm or of events on Earth before the subject was conceived. Those types of memories naturally are less likely to be corroborated. Though the descriptions of another realm may well be fantasy, when we evaluate such claims, we should keep them in context with other statements that the child has made that have been verified.

We may also want to question why so few of the subjects in our cases talk about the time between lives. If the children are remembering previous lives, then we might expect them all to have memories of the time between the lives as well. In some ways, the issue seems absurd, in that we are talking about fairly incredible statements and then wondering why we do not hear more of them, but we may logically ask how a child could remember a previous life but lose memories of events after that.

One possibility is that memories from the time between lives are less likely to make an imprint on a developing brain if they were not associated with a brain when they were originally acquired. Memories of events that take place between lives, other than ones from time in the womb, would obviously have to be stored in something other than a brain. That other something, that consciousness, might carry memories of the previous life to the next one. Though it might also store memories of events that occur between lives, those new memories would be unlikely to imprint on a developing brain since they did not come from a brain in the first place.

Regardless of the cause, we can say that only a minority of children who claim past-life memories also report remembering events that took place between the end of that life and their own births. Their reports are intriguing and in some cases have been verified, at least partially, to be accurate.

CHAPTER 9

Opposing Points of View

Critics have challenged the concept of reincarnation in various ways, and in this chapter, we will look at the main arguments they have made. If they are convincing enough, then we may have to question whether we should even consider the evidence of the cases. After all, if we know that the idea of reincarnation is impossible, then we do not need to devote a lot of energy into looking at work that suggests that it happens. I do not need to spend much time studying a mathematical proof that shows that $1=2$ if I know for a fact that $1 \neq 2$. On the other hand, I may feel very sure about something but, when I look carefully, find that I am mistaken. To quote an old line, "The trouble with people is not that they don't know but that they know so much that ain't so." The question for us is whether the certainty that some people feel in rejecting the concept of reincarnation is based on fact or on things that just ain't so.

In looking at the arguments, I will not focus on the criticisms of the various religious beliefs that are associated with reincarnation, since those beliefs are not the basis of the work in this book. The research does not assume that they are correct and, as we will discuss in Chapter 10, does not necessarily support them. It considers the possibility of reincarnation in its most basic form—that the consciousness of an individual can survive after the person dies and then continue in a future individual.

Before beginning this discussion, I want to quote a noted skeptic. Carl Sagan, the popular astronomer, was a founding member of a debunking organization, the Committee for the Scientific Investigation of Claims of the Paranormal (CSICOP). In 1996, he wrote a book called *The Demon-Haunted World* in which he was extremely critical of many New Age or paranormal ideas. In it, he also wrote, "At the time of writing there are three claims in the [parapsychology] field which, in my opinion, deserve serious study," with the third being "that young children sometimes report details of a previous life, which upon checking turn out to be accurate and which they could not have known about in any other way than reincarnation." He was not saying that he believed in reincarnation, because he did not, but he thought that we should take this work seriously.

Do we have reasons for ignoring that opinion? Let us find out.

The Materialist Worldview

In the scientific world, the primary criticism of reincarnation is that it cannot happen because the material world is all that exists. In such a view, consciousness is only the result of a functioning brain, and it cannot exist independently from one. Thus, consciousness ends when the brain dies. Scientists say that they know this, either because the idea of survival after death conflicts too much with what we know about the materialist nature of the world or because there is no evidence that it happens.

Recently, a number of respected scientists, mainly physicists, have put forth views in several areas that, taken together, challenge this materialist dismissal of consciousness as being merely an insignificant byproduct of a functioning brain. Different groups have argued that we should consider consciousness separate from the brain, that modern physics can incorporate paranormal phenomena, and even that consciousness is an essential part of the universe. Though none of these arguments deals directly with reincarnation, we will see how they could be part of a new overall understanding of the universe in which consciousness is a key player rather than just an insignificant byproduct of the brain. Such an understanding may eventually allow the idea of an independently functioning consciousness to become part of our scientific knowledge.

The idea that consciousness can be considered separately from the brain is in many ways at the crux of the question of reincarnation, and it has been present for centuries. Descartes developed the concept of dualism in the 1600s to separate mind—the world of thoughts—from matter, including the brain. With it, he argued that an immaterial world, the world of thoughts, existed along with the material world. If the immaterial mind is separate from the matter of the brain, then this raises the question of whether it can exist after the brain dies.

Many mainstream scientists would say that the idea that the immaterial substance of the mind could interact with the material of the brain is nonsensical, and some go so far as to say that the concept of dualism violates known laws of physics. If the mind is to affect the body, then it must change a physical entity, namely the brain cells, even though it has no physical energy or mass associated with it. Such a change requires an expenditure of energy. Since no source of energy is available, the process would violate the principle of the conservation of energy. As one critic has written, "this confrontation between quite standard physics and dualism has been endlessly discussed since Descartes's own day, and is widely regarded as the inescapable and fatal flaw of dualism."

In response to this, physicist Henry Stapp has written, "This argument depends on identifying 'standard physics' with nineteenth century physics. But the argument collapses when one goes over to contemporary physics, . . . in which conscious effort can influence brain activity without violating the laws of physics. Contemporary physical theory allows, and in its orthodox von Neumann form entails, an interactive dualism." In his model, consciousness can produce effects, "yet it is fully compatible with all known laws of physics, including the law of conservation of energy." When he says contemporary physics, he is referring to quantum mechanics, the understanding of the physical world at the microscopic level of molecules, atoms, and subatomic particles. Likewise, John C. Eccles, a Nobel Prize–winning neuroscientist, advanced a dualist solution to the problem. He and quantum physicist Friedrich Beck hypothesized a mechanism using quantum mechanics for how the mind could act on the brain without violating the laws of conservation, and this involved mental intention affecting the brain by increasing the probabilities for the release of chemicals, called neurotransmitters, into the junctions between nerve cells.

In the area of physics and paranormal phenomena, some physicists have challenged the idea that the two are incompatible. Elizabeth Rauscher and Russell Targ have argued that the usual four dimensions of time and space cannot incorporate the findings of parapsychological research, but that a geometrical model of space-time known as "complex Minkowski space" can be used successfully to describe the major findings of parapsychology. On the other hand, O. Costa de Beauregard has challenged the idea that the geometrical time-space idea is even necessary to explain psychic phenomena. He has written that the occurrence of the paranormal phenomena is clearly implied by theoretical physics and that precognition, telepathy, and psychokinesis are allowed by its laws. In fact, he has written that "far from being 'irrational,' *the paranormal is postulated by today's physics*." Brian Josephson, a Nobel Prize–winning physicist, created controversy when he contributed a short piece for a booklet that accompanied a set of stamps that the Royal Mail issued in Great Britain to commemorate the 100th anniversary of the Nobel Prizes. In it, he wrote that quantum theory was now being combined with theories of information and computation and that "these developments may lead to an explanation of processes still not understood within conventional science, such as telepathy." He has written that he thinks that in the long run, such phenomena as telepathy and mind-matter interactions, which I will discuss shortly, will be accepted and confirmed by science.

In the area of the importance of consciousness in the universe, experiments have demonstrated that with subatomic particles, several potential realities can be present at the same time until observation forces them to be limited to one possibility. This can be a difficult concept to comprehend, so here is an example. In a classic experiment called a double slit experiment, light particles, or photons, act like waves, appearing to spread out and go through two slits at once, unless physicists set up detectors beside the slits that record the individual photons as they pass through. In that case, each photon goes through one slit or the other but not both, giving the impression that the observation forces the photons down one path or the other.

John Wheeler, an important physicist who, among many other achievements, gave black holes their name, has extended this concept to demonstrate how conscious observers in the present can affect events in the past. He developed a thought experiment that showed that measurements made now by astronomers on Earth could affect the path that a particle of light from a faraway quasar had taken for billions of years before the astronomers made their observations. The experiment later was demonstrated in principle in a laboratory. Wheeler thinks that on a quantum level the universe is a work in progress in which not only the future is still undetermined but the past is as well, and conscious observers are one factor that can help select one out of many possible quantum pasts for the universe. Andrei Linde, a Stanford University physicist, goes even further and says that conscious observers are an essential component of the universe. He says, "I cannot imagine a consistent theory of everything [the goal in physics to have a unified theory of the universe that explains both the large-scale universe of gravity and relativity and the small-scale universe of quantum mechanics] that ignores consciousness."

When we combine the ideas of these well-respected scientists—that we should consider consciousness separate from the brain, that modern physics can be used to explain paranormal phenomena, and that consciousness is an essential part of the universe—we get a view of consciousness that is very different from the materialist dismissal of it. Consciousness is an essential and independent force in the universe in this view, and the parapsychological effects that it might be expected to produce are consistent with current understandings in physics. If this view is correct, we should be able to find evidence beyond what our cases provide that supports the idea of consciousness functioning independently from a brain.

Other Pieces of Evidence

In fact, researchers in several areas have produced evidence that consciousness is not confined to an individual brain. Research indicates that a person's consciousness or mental effort can produce effects on objects or living things that are in a different location from the person, meaning that the consciousness has had an effect some distance away from the person's brain. One group of studies has looked at whether people can influence the functioning of physical systems using only their minds—this is called mind-matter interactions. In these studies, subjects use their minds to attempt to change the output of machines called random number generators so that the outputs are no longer random. This is like trying to influence the outcome of coin flips with your mind so that heads comes up more than half of the time. This research has produced a mountain of data showing a small but significant effect. One large review looked at more than 800 studies conducted by sixty-eight different researchers and determined that "it is difficult to avoid the conclusion that under certain circumstances, consciousness interacts with random physical systems."

Another group of studies has looked at the effect that mental intention can have on other living organisms. This area is known as Direct Mental Interaction with Living Systems or DMILS. Researchers have conducted dozens of studies looking at the ability of subjects to affect the rates of various processes, including, among others, plant growth, recovery of animals from anesthesia, growth of tumors in animals, wound healing in animals, and the growth of yeasts and bacteria. At last count, out of 191 controlled studies that had been done, eighty-three had produced results that were statistically significant to the point that the likelihood of their being due to chance was less than one in a hundred, and another forty-one had results that would occur by chance only two to five times out of a hundred. Where we might expect no more than a handful of studies to be positive by chance, 124 of them recorded positive results.

Some studies have looked specifically at whether one person's consciousness can produce health benefits in another person by having subjects try to improve the condition of patients either through prayer or, more generally, through what is known as distant healing. As the name suggests, distant healing is the practice of attempting to improve another person's health using only mental effort while being apart from that person. In these studies, the patients have not known whether subjects were attempting prayer or distant healing for them. The studies have shown positive results for such conditions as heart disease and AIDS. One review found that out of twenty-three studies, thirteen showed statistically significant treatment effects, which is far above what we would expect by chance.

All of these studies, whether with machines, living organisms, or patients, suggest that consciousness can have an effect at a distance from the brain. Though this is not the same as saying that consciousness survives after the brain dies, if consciousness can act in a way that is physically separate from the brain, we have to wonder if it can operate separated in time from a functioning brain as well.

Does other evidence exist to support the idea of consciousness continuing after a patient dies? One area of research into this question is the field of near-death experiences. Many people who survive an incident in which they come very close to death or are clinically dead for a short period of time report experiences that they had during that time. These often involve an impression of leaving their bodies and witnessing events from above and then going to another realm where they meet deceased relatives or religious beings. Much of this is subjective, of course, and cannot be proven, but some people have reported hearing or seeing events take place below them during the near-death experience that were later verified to have happened.

One of these, Pam Reynolds, accurately described medical equipment that was not visible while she was awake and a conversation that took place in the operating room while she was unconscious during surgery for a brain aneurysm in which her body was cooled to 60 degrees, her heart was stopped, and the blood was drained from her body. In another example, Dr. Bruce Greyson here at the University of Virginia investigated the report by a man named Al Sullivan about his experiences during an emergency coronary bypass operation. He said that when he looked down on the scene during his near-death experience, he saw his surgeon flapping his elbows. The surgeon and Mr. Sullivan's cardiologist confirmed to Dr. Greyson that the surgeon does have the unusual habit of flapping his elbows after scrubbing in for surgery.

Another area of research focuses on reports of apparitions, which are accounts by people of being visited by individuals who are not physically present. Studies of these began in the late 1800s. They can involve individuals who are either living or deceased, and some have included visits by individuals at the time of their death, even though the person who witnessed the apparition had no reason to think that the individual was dying. In a number of the reports, people have described learning details about the nature of the death that they could not have known at the time. Collective cases have also occurred in which more than one person saw the apparition appear.

Research with mediums, individuals who claim to communicate with the dead, also began in the late 1800s. Though some mediums have either been exposed as frauds or have been found to give no information that they could not have inferred through normal means, some gifted individuals, who have been carefully studied, have been able to demonstrate specific and personal knowledge about sitters—those who come to them for readings—and their deceased loved ones. One such medium, Mrs. Leonora Piper, was first studied by William James, the early American psychologist, in the 1880s. She was also taken to England and studied by the Society for Psychical Research. Investigators went to great lengths to guard against fraud by using such measures as having detectives follow her for weeks to make sure that she was not trying to find out information about potential sitters. In that context, she produced intimate material in remarkable detail about the strangers who came for readings. Mrs. Osborne Leonard, a British medium in the early twentieth century, was similarly studied and proved to be similarly impressive. She demonstrated a particular ability to provide information that was unknown to sitters at the time and was later verified to be accurate.

In recent times, mediumship has practically become a cottage industry with a number of mediums becoming television personalities. While this new group has not been investigated with the intensity that Mrs. Piper and Mrs. Leonard were, some have participated in recent studies, and other studies are ongoing.

Each of these fields has weaknesses along with strengths, but when you consider them as a group, you may wonder why mainstream science has ignored all the evidence that this research has produced. Science is very conservative, and its stability rests on the idea that new understandings of the world must fit in with the previous knowledge about it. Biologist E. O. Wilson has used the term "consilience" to describe this, the "jumping together" of knowledge when facts and theories from different areas link and form a common foundation of knowledge. As he says, "the explanations of different phenomena most likely to survive are those that can be connected and proved consistent with one another."

Though such a view is undoubtedly true, it can lead mainstream science to favor strongly the status quo for as long as possible, unable at times to accept new knowledge that will later look completely obvious. The history of the field is filled with unfortunate examples in which mainstream science turned its back on large amounts of evidence that challenged conventional wisdom. These go back at least as far as Galileo, who had to go before the Inquisition in 1633 for advocating the idea that the earth revolved around the sun.

Other particularly infamous examples include the failure of scientists to recognize the existence of meteorites despite reports by farmers of rocks falling from the sky into their fields. Scientists considered such an idea to be ridiculous—how could stones fall from the sky when there are no stones in the sky? Then there was poor Ignaz Semmelweis, an obstetrician in the 1800s who died in a mental institution at the age of forty-seven after he was vilified for producing data that showed that death rates during childbirth dropped significantly if doctors washed their hands before examining patients.

In the twentieth century, Alfred Wegener's idea of continental drift was initially ridiculed, despite considerable evidence to support it, because as one geologist put it, "If we are to believe Wegener's hypothesis, we must forget everything which has been learned in the last seventy years and start all over again." His theory languished for decades before it became the premise for the currently accepted idea of plate tectonics.

Mainstream science, of course, has rightly rejected many kooky ideas. Determining which ideas should be considered and which should be rejected can be difficult. The conservative nature of science has been its biggest strength and its biggest weakness. The basic understanding of the world tends to change at a pace that is almost as slow as continental drift, but the reluctance to accept new ideas too readily keeps that understanding from bouncing back and forth haphazardly. The need for consilience—the ability of new knowledge to be woven into the fabric of current understanding—helps to filter out erroneous beliefs, but it can also keep new insights from being accepted.

The question for us is whether the idea of reincarnation could ever be consilient with what we know, or think we know, about the world in general. One problem is that we do not have an adequate theory to explain how reincarnation might work. We only have the outlines of a theory, based on the notion that consciousness is not confined to the brain. The consciousness in a particular individual continues to exist after that person dies and then can attach itself to a developing fetus, bringing memories, emotions, and even traumas with it.

Though such a concept conflicts with a materialistic view of the world, when we consider the evidence for a separate and surviving consciousness I have described along with the recent ideas put forth by physicists, we can see that a blanket statement that anything that conflicts with a materialist view of the universe must be false risks becoming considered one day as shortsighted as the past rejections by mainstream science of phenomena such as meteorites do now. The field of quantum mechanics may provide a model for how a world of consciousness could become consilient with our other knowledge. The world of the universe's smallest particles has rules that are very different from the larger world that is made up of those particles, leading scientists to speak of quantum weirdness, but the field of quantum mechanics has been accepted alongside our understandings of the larger universe. Similarly, the rules of the world of consciousness may be very different from the rules of the material universe, but this would not preclude its acceptance as part of the universe as a whole. We will need to understand more about consciousness before most mainstream scientists would accept reincarnation, but the positions of well-respected scientists suggest that consilience might one day be possible.

Unknown Mechanisms

An argument along lines similar to the materialist one is that we should not consider reincarnation as a possibility, because we do not know of a mechanism that could explain it—we do not know how a consciousness might survive without a body, how it could affect a developing fetus, and so on. The weakness of this argument is fairly obvious on the face of it, but even more so when we consider it in other contexts. We are fortunate that the field of medicine has not waited for mechanisms to be uncovered before taking advantage of effective treatments, since physicians have successfully used numerous medications before knowing their mechanisms of action.

The mechanism of gravity was a complete mystery at the time that Isaac Newton proposed the concept, but people accepted its existence nonetheless. We did not have a mechanism to explain it until Albert Einstein proposed in his general theory of relativity that gravity is the warping of space and time. This case demonstrates that even arguing that no mechanism is conceivable is not enough to reject an idea since the warping of space and time was certainly an inconceivable idea when Newton proposed the concept of gravity. Unless we are willing to say that we know that no mechanism is even possible, we should not dismiss a concept simply because we do not know its mechanism.

The Population Explosion

Some have argued that population growth rules out reincarnation as a possibility. Their reasoning goes that the increase in the numbers of humans in modern times means that all the individuals currently alive could not have been reincarnating through multiple past lives, because the modern population is so much larger than populations in the past. A number of objections undercut this argument. In the first place, reincarnation does not have to happen to everyone. Some might get reborn because of "unfinished business" from their previous lives or because of the manner of their deaths or some other factor, but others might not get reborn. Some modern individuals would possess previous lives even if most would not. We also have no reason to think that new individuals could not be created, so again, even if all individuals have multiple lifetimes, some people who are currently alive could have had past lives while others would be here for the first time. In either of these situations, the number of individuals living at a given time would be irrelevant.

David Bishai of the Johns Hopkins School of Public Health has shown that we do not even need these scenarios to explain reincarnation in the presence of population growth. He looked at the question of how many humans have ever lived on Earth. Estimates are required, of course, since we do not know a lot about the size of the human population in ancient times, and a judgment has to made about which of our early ancestors we should consider human. Dr. Bishai quotes a calculation using a start date for human existence of 50,000 B.C.E. that estimated that 105 billion human beings have lived on Earth. Since population growth is predicted to max out at around ten billion people later this century, the number of humans in the past is certainly big enough to allow for reincarnation. Dr. Bishai does point out that the average amount of time between lives would have to shorten to accommodate the increase in population. We have no reason, of course, to think that the average amount of time between lives would have to remain constant, so population growth does not rule out reincarnation.

Alzheimer's Disease

Another argument is that the loss of memory and personality that comes with the brain deterioration of Alzheimer's disease shows that an intact brain is necessary for consciousness to occur. If memories and personality features cannot survive the partial destruction of the brain, they surely cannot survive death. In considering this, we can acknowledge that a person certainly needs an intact brain to express memories and personality, but that does not necessarily mean that the brain is producing those things. William James looked at this question in the late 1800s in relation to the overall question of life after death. He suggested that the brain, rather than producing thoughts, might permit or transmit them. In this transmission theory, he likened the brain to a colored glass that sifts and limits the color of light that passes through it, even though it does not produce the light itself. He pointed out that though consciousness depends on the brain to transmit it in the natural world, this dependence could be quite compatible with the possibility of its continuing supernaturally after the end of a life. He said that when the brain decays or stops altogether, the stream of consciousness associated with it vanishes from this natural world, but the "sphere of being" that supplied that consciousness could still be intact.

I do not know if James would have approved of the following analogy, but we can consider the modern example of the television. If your television breaks, the stream of images it supplied is no longer present for you to enjoy, but since it simply transmitted those images instead of creating them, the television programs continue to exist until you find another television to bring those images to life in your home. Similarly, the consciousness that found expression in the natural world through a particular brain may continue after that brain decays or dies, and it may then associate with a new brain, a new transmitter, at a later date.

Though this line of reasoning does not prove that such a phenomenon actually happens, James pointed out that the idea that the brain produces consciousness out of nothing is no more simple or credible in itself than any other theory, such as the proposal that it is an organ that transmits consciousness. Indeed, science has made little more progress today in pinpointing a source of consciousness in the brain than it had in James's day 100 years ago.

Another "argument" that some people make against reincarnation is simply that the idea is absurd. Well, ridicule is a poor substitute for reasoned discussion. The important issue is to determine what it is about reincarnation that would make it absurd. I believe that I have addressed the strongest scientific and logical criticisms of reincarnation, and I do not see any reason to reject it out of hand.

Religious Objections

At the other end of the spectrum, some people object to the idea of reincarnation because it conflicts with their religious beliefs. Addressing this objection in a scientific way is not possible since it is not a scientific objection, but it is still an issue that warrants consideration. Those making the objection tend to have Judeo-Christian beliefs, so we will look at those religions.

Although reincarnation is not a part of mainstream Judeo-Christian doctrine, some members of those religions have believed in it. Many in the West today believe in reincarnation as individuals, and some Judeo-Christian groups have included reincarnation in their beliefs. In Judaism, the Kabbalah includes reincarnation, which is also a part of the Hasidic Jewish belief system. Some groups of early Christians, particularly the Gnostic Christians, believed in reincarnation, and some Christians in southern Europe believed in it until the Second Council of Constantinople in 553 C.E. Exactly what happened at that meeting has been a source of controversy, but church leaders there were believed to have condemned the idea of souls existing before conception.

The Bible contains passages in the New Testament that seem to refer to reincarnation. In Matthew 11:10–14 and 17:10–13, Jesus says that John the Baptist is the prophet Elijah who had lived centuries before, and he does not appear to be speaking metaphorically. Some point out in response to this that Elijah did not die according to the Old Testament, but ascended to heaven in a whirlwind, so he would have been returning to Earth rather than being reborn. The Gospel of Luke contradicts this line of reasoning in describing John the Baptist's birth, beginning life as a baby and not as a mature prophet returned to Earth.

Another possible allusion to reincarnation takes place when the disciples ask Jesus in John 9:2 whether a particular man was born blind because of his sins or those of his parents. This obviously implies that they thought the man had an opportunity to sin before he was born, suggesting a previous existence. In response, Jesus does not reject that possibility but says that the man was born blind so that the works of God could be manifest in him, and proceeds to cure the blindness.

Beyond these specific passages, we should consider whether reincarnation conflicts with Judeo-Christian doctrines in general. The existence of reincarnation would mean that we have not had a full understanding of life after death. Many other religious issues are not clear-cut either. The Bible is open to multiple interpretations, as the different views of the various denominations make clear. The Bible does not spell out the concept of reincarnation to be sure, but that does not mean that reincarnation necessarily conflicts with what is in the Bible. In fact, it does not even necessarily conflict with the concepts of heaven and hell, since some people with a belief in reincarnation, including some Shiite Muslim groups, believe that an ultimate Judgment Day comes after a series of lives, when God sends souls to heaven or hell based on the moral quality of their actions during all their various lives.

In addition, the doctrine of reincarnation would certainly not conflict with the value given to love and kindness by the Judeo-Christian religions as well as the other major world religions. It does nothing to change the idea that living a loving, ethical life is important, whether it is a single life or one in a series.

In summary, we have looked at various criticisms of reincarnation, and we have seen that any certainty that people feel about the impossibility of reincarnation is not justified. We have looked at some objections—for example, the claims that there is no evidence of survival after death, and that population growth rules out reincarnation—and seen that they just ain't so. We have also seen that none of the other criticisms justifies ignoring evidence that supports it. None of them makes believing in the possibility of reincarnation resemble believing that 1 = 2. We do not have an adequate reason to reject the concept and this body of work out of hand. As Carl Sagan wrote, we need to study seriously the evidence that this work has produced.

CHAPTER 10

Conclusions and Speculations

To review the possible explanations for this phenomenon, the best normal explanation in the cases with birthmarks and birth defects involves coincidence for the birthmarks and faulty memory by informants for the statements that the children make. In the cases that primarily involve statements by the child, knowledge acquired through normal means can be used for cases in which the previous personality either was a family member of the subject or lived in the same village, and faulty memory by informants is the best normal explanation for most of the others. It is clearly not sufficient, however, for the cases with written records that were made of the child's statements before the previous personality was identified, so we have to resort to fraud as a way to explain those. The best normal explanations for the past-life behaviors of the children are fantasy combined with coincidence and faulty memory by informants, but they both have weaknesses. Finally, in the cases with recognitions by the children, we can use faulty memory by informants to explain many of them, but we are again left with fraud as the only normal explanation possible for the controlled recognition tests.

Since faulty memory by informants provides the best normal explanation for many of the cases, I want to present a couple of studies that have looked at that possibility. In the first one, Dr. Stevenson and Dr. Keil compared reports that the families made about cases at different times. The study began when Dr. Keil unintentionally restudied several cases that Dr. Stevenson had studied twenty years before. He then intentionally reinvestigated more of Dr. Stevenson's earlier ones until he had studied fifteen of them. He did this to see if the reports by the families had become exaggerated over time. After all, the whole idea behind the faulty memory by informants possibility is that the families are crediting the children with more specific knowledge about the previous lives than they actually demonstrated before the two families met, so Dr. Keil wanted to see if the claims had grown following the original reports that the families gave to Dr. Stevenson.

When Dr. Keil interviewed the families, he did not know what information they had originally given to Dr. Stevenson. Even after he began intentionally restudying cases, he only had the names and addresses of the subjects whose cases Dr. Stevenson had investigated years before. He then went to the families and made notes of the new interviews that he had with them. Once he completed his investigation, he and Dr. Stevenson compared the information that he got with what Dr. Stevenson had obtained years before. Given the time that had elapsed, the investigations were not identical, and in some cases, the people that Dr. Keil interviewed differed somewhat from the ones available to Dr. Stevenson twenty years before.

When Dr. Keil and Dr. Stevenson reviewed the information that each of them had collected, they found that only one of the cases had become stronger based on what the witnesses said. In that case, the subject's family described an incident to Dr. Keil that they had not mentioned to Dr. Stevenson that involved the subject finding a special spoon that the previous personality, the subject's deceased brother, had kept on a high shelf in a fairly inaccessible place.

In three other cases, the strength of the reports basically remained the same. Some of the details were different in one report compared to the other, but overall, the cases had not grown stronger or weaker over time. The reports of the other eleven cases had actually become weaker by the time that Dr. Keil talked with the families. This was often because the informants gave fewer details than they had given to Dr. Stevenson years before. This is logical, of course, since we generally remember fewer details about events as time goes on, but in this situation, it is also important. It shows that the cases do not grow stronger in people's minds over time, and in fact, these had become weaker over time. As we have seen, a number of the cases include features that tempt us to conclude that witnesses must be remembering statements or events incorrectly. This study does not provide any support for such a conclusion.

Dr. Sybo Schouten and Dr. Stevenson conducted the other study that looked at this question. They compared cases in which written records were made of the children's statements before the families met with cases that did not include such records. They were testing the idea that the parents exaggerate the statements that the child made about the previous personality before the families met. They expected that if this were true, the cases in which written records document what the children actually said before the families met would include fewer statements and fewer correct ones than the cases without such records.

Since the cases with written records have come mainly from

India and Sri Lanka, Drs. Schouten and Stevenson looked at all thoroughly investigated cases from those two countries in which the number of correct and incorrect statements had been determined and recorded. This produced twenty-one cases with written records made before the families met and eighty-two cases without, and they then compared the two groups. What they found was surprising. The average number of statements in the cases with the written records was twenty-five and a half, while the average in the cases without the records was significantly lower, at eighteen and a half. The percentage of correct statements was essentially the same in both groups—76.7 percent in the written record cases and 78.4 percent in the cases without records.

Thus, the findings of the study are the opposite of what we would expect if because of faulty memory the informants were crediting the children with more (and more correct) statements than they had actually made before the families met. In the cases without written records, they were crediting the children with fewer statements, presumably because they had forgotten some of the statements since no one had written them down. As Drs. Schouten and Stevenson point out, the findings show that if the families do credit the children with more knowledge about the previous life than they actually demonstrated before the families met, they do not do so enough to affect the data in a measurable way.

This study meshes well with the results of the previous one in that it indicates that the reports in the cases grow less detailed over time rather than more, since informants in the cases without written records remembered fewer statements by the children than the number documented in the cases with written records.

This is consistent with the finding of Drs. Stevenson and Keil that many cases become weaker over time. Taken together, these two studies really cast doubt on the proposition that the main cause of the cases is that witnesses incorrectly remember the children's statements about the previous life as being more impressive than they really were. If this were the case, we would expect the reports to become stronger over the years as the memories of the witnesses become less accurate, when in fact the reports frequently become weaker, and we would expect the cases that include written documentation of what the children actually said to have fewer statements and fewer correct ones, when they actually have more statements and the same percentage of correct ones.

Given that faulty memory by informants is the primary normal explanation for many of the cases, this leaves us without a solid way of explaining them through normal means. Of course, as we have already seen, no single normal explanation can explain all the different types of cases, but having grave doubt cast over the most common explanation is especially challenging.

Since no single explanation can explain all the cases, the only feasible way at this point to explain them through normal means is to say that a normal process produces each case through some imperfection in the case, and different processes are responsible for different cases. In considering this, we should first note that no perfect case exists. Perfection is rarely found in science—for any medical study that is done, someone can always find a way to criticize it or to doubt its findings. This is particularly true in the study of spontaneous phenomena. These cases do not take place in a laboratory where we can control all of the conditions to produce the cleanest cases possible. Instead, they take place in the real world of uncontrolled conditions. Some phenomena occur in nature and cannot be reproduced in a lab, and if we think that they are important enough to study, then we have to accept the limitations that come with that.

Therefore, none of these cases is perfect, and we recognize that. With the imperfections, we can argue that a dishonest set of parents here or a coincidence there or a conversation about the previous life in front of a young child or else bad memory can explain each case, so perhaps together they can explain all the cases.

Is such an explanation satisfactory? In a particular case, we may think, for example, that coincidence is quite unlikely but nonetheless possible. If we use such reasoning to explain all 2,500 cases, then we are taking the unlikely and raising it to extremes. After a while, looking for any conceivable defect in each individual case begins to feel like missing the forest for the trees. If we stand back and look at this worldwide phenomenon as a whole, then we see a pattern of remarkable events. Even though the cases are only evidence and not "proof" of a paranormal process, when we consider the weaknesses of the normal explanations, I do not think that they can adequately explain the strongest cases as a group. I think they fail, and therefore, we must turn to the paranormal possibilities to see if they can provide a better explanation.

When we look at the different types of cases all together, reincarnation provides a much more straightforward explanation overall than either ESP or possession. It easily explains all of the cases, which the others do not do, and it certainly is a more obvious explanation than the other two. The big question becomes whether the cases provide enough evidence of a paranormal process so that we should favor reincarnation over the normal explanations.

Dr. Stevenson has written that he has become persuaded that "reincarnation is the best—even though not the only—explanation for the stronger cases we have investigated." To be slightly more conservative, I would say that the best explanation for the strongest cases is that memories, emotions, and even physical injuries can sometimes carry over from one life to the next. If this is what we mean by reincarnation, then my conclusion is the same as Dr. Stevenson's, but since, as he has also written, we know almost nothing about reincarnation, I prefer to use the more specific terminology.

While this may seem to be an astounding statement—that memories, emotions, and physical injuries can sometimes carry over from one life to the next—the evidence, I think, leads us to that conclusion. It is no more astounding than many currently accepted ideas in physics seemed to be when they were originally proposed, and since the evidence has led us to it, we need to consider it. I fully acknowledge that I may be wrong—as Dr. Stevenson wrote, this is the best explanation of the cases but not the only one—but the skeptics may be wrong as well, whether they admit it or not. Though such skeptics would obviously make a different determination, the idea of reincarnation or carry-over from one life to the next appears to be the best conclusion based on the evidence that this research has produced over the last forty years. If this means that we need to question some of our materialistic assumptions about how the world works, then so be it.

In attempting to understand this, we should keep in mind that some physicists now consider consciousness to be an entity separate from the brain and one with important functions in the universe.

Conscious observation, at least, appears capable of affecting the future and even the past on the level of the microscopic quantum world, and if consciousness is indeed a fundamental part of the universe—if Stanford physicist Andrei Linde is correct when he says that a consistent theory of everything that ignores consciousness is unimaginable—then the world is a far more complex and wondrous place than what the physical world shows us in everyday life.

In physics, concepts in relativity and quantum mechanics have already shown us that the universe as we currently understand it is far different from what our everyday experience tells us about it. Similarly, most of us are only aware of our own consciousness, and we process that awareness with our individual brains. This may cause us to have trouble fully accepting evidence that consciousness is a factor in the universe beyond what seems to be occurring in our individual brains. If consciousness is a fundamental part of the universe, then we have to consider whether we can logically decide that it is simply a byproduct of functioning brains. If conscious observation can determine the path that a particle of light took billions of years ago, as John Wheeler has proposed, then does it make sense that consciousness just happened to develop as a temporary state of a functioning human brain? I think not. We may assume that a fundamental component of the universe, if that is what consciousness is, exists separately from our little brains here on Earth. Even though our everyday experience may tell us that our consciousness begins with our birth and ends with our death, a reasonable alternative is that our brains serve as vehicles for consciousness during our lifetimes, and that consciousness existed before our births and can continue after our deaths until it finds another vehicle in a new body.

The evidence in our cases supports this idea, and for the remainder of this chapter, we will operate from the perspective that if this is true, we can consider what the cases may tell us about the process of reincarnation. We will have to speculate a fair amount as we do so, and we should remember that the world of consciousness may operate very differently from the physical universe. Therefore, any conclusions that we make about reincarnation are tentative at this point, but we have some fascinating questions to explore.

Does Everybody Reincarnate?

When we see evidence for reincarnation, one reaction is to think about how it could affect us individually. Clearly, we would all love the opportunity to see our deceased loved ones again. We can think about the emotions that Patrick Christenson's mother must have felt when she determined that her first son, who had died as a toddler, had returned to her. A loss of that kind is obviously devastating, and we would all be comforted to know that such a loss might not be permanent.

Unfortunately, we must remember that what is true about the children who report past-life memories may not be true for the rest of us. They may be a unique group, and even if they have reincarnated, no one else may have. For instance, they may have had issues that kept them connected to their earthly experiences so that they came back while others do not. The situation could be like stories of haunted houses in which people say that a ghost is stuck there because of a grisly death or a similar reason. As I discussed earlier, 70 percent of the previous personalities died by unnatural means in cases where the mode of death is known, and of course a number of those dying by natural means died suddenly as well. This suggests that a violent or sudden death is much more likely to produce a future case of a child with past-life memories than other types of deaths. Such a death may be one factor that can cause our subjects to have connections to the Earth that lead them to be exceptions to the normal state of affairs. After death, the consciousness may typically blend into a larger universal consciousness or go off to another realm of existence—heaven, for example. For all we know, the traditional Judeo-Christian views of life after death may be correct in general even if our cases are legitimate examples of reincarnation.

On the other hand, reincarnation may normally occur but without memories continuing from the previous life. In that case, we may all have had previous lives even though most of us do not remember them. If this is true, then the usual process may get disrupted either by a factor in the previous life like an unexpected death or by some factor in the next life. This may lead some memories to be present in the next life, and therefore, even though everyone may reincarnate, our cases are unusual because of the presence of the memories.

The cases do not answer which possibility is more likely, past lives being unusual or just the memories of past lives being unusual, even though they indicate that reincarnation occurs in some circumstances. Although we would all like either to see our deceased loved ones return to us, or to return ourselves to our children or grandchildren after our deaths, these cases do not answer the question of whether reincarnation is universal. They provide evidence that we *can* reincarnate, at least under certain circumstances—which is certainly a significant finding—but they do not indicate if all of us actually do.

Even if we all do reincarnate, the patterns we see in the cases with memories may not apply to the rest of us. The type of death or some other factor might change the normal process to produce patterns that could go along with the enduring memories. For instance, the children who have past-life memories may be more connected to a certain location than others would be. These children tend to reincarnate close to where the previous personality lived, yet others who reincarnate without memories may not be similarly constrained. Likewise, the children who describe staying in one particular location for years between lives may not be typical of all who reincarnate. We should remember that other differences could occur as well between the cases of children who have past-life memories and any others who reincarnate without such memories.

In Cases of Reincarnation, What Reincarnates?

Despite these reservations, we should still examine these cases closely to see what they say about life after death. One question is this: If these cases are examples of reincarnation, then exactly what reincarnates? The cases show that memories, emotions, and physical traumas can carry over to a future life. I have referred to a consciousness continuing, but this is not a very specific term. Other terms that can be used, such as "soul" or "astral body," have connotations we may not feel are accurate. For that reason,

Dr. Stevenson coined the term "psychophore," which he derived from the Greek meaning "soul bearing," to describe the vehicle that would carry the memories after a death.

This entity, the psychophore or consciousness, appears to be able to obtain new information, based on cases in which the children describe events that occurred after the previous personality died. We might wonder how it could do so, since the consciousness obviously does not have sense organs like eyes and ears. The answer must be that it can get information through paranormal means. This is similar to the reports of patients who have near-death experiences, as they often describe watching events from above their bodies. It also fits with other studies in parapsychology that show some people are able to gain knowledge that they do not obtain through their normal sense organs. Rather, they gain it through paranormal means, and though we do not know what those means are, if a person can do so during a life, then we can logically assume that their consciousness could do so if it survives death.

While we tend to think that reincarnation means that some entity has continued from one life to the next, many Buddhists, particularly Theravada Buddhists, say that this is not the case. Their doctrine of *anatta,* or "no soul," emphasizes that there is no "self" and thus no entity that continues from one life to the next. At the death of one personality, a new one comes into being, much as the flame of a dying candle can serve to light the flame of another. Continuity between personalities occurs, because the karmic forces that the previous person sets in motion lead to the subsequent rebirth, but no identity persists. Since I am far from a Buddhist scholar, I confess that I have trouble embracing or even fully understanding this concept, but I can at least note that despite this doctrine, most practicing Buddhists do, in fact, believe that an actual entity gets reborn.

As Dr. Stevenson notes, our cases certainly suggest that some vehicle has carried the enduring memories with it to the next life. Something more seems to have survived than just the memories and emotions. We have talked about how the birthmarks might arise when the consciousness is so traumatized by the injuries in one life that it then affects the developing fetus to produce similar marks on the new body. I have trouble imagining that such a process could take place without *something,* whether we call it a consciousness or a psychophore or some other term, carrying the effects of the injury on to the next life. Though some Buddhists would no doubt disagree, our cases imply that some entity, which I have called a consciousness, can continue from one life to the next.

The fact that physical trauma can affect the consciousness to such a degree that it produces marks on the developing fetus implies that this consciousness can affect the physical body. This goes back to our discussion of dualism in Chapter 9 and the question of whether immaterial thoughts can affect the material world, in this case the developing fetus. These cases suggest that they can. In addition, the cases show that the mind itself can be affected by traumatic events. We discussed cases in Chapter 4 in which patients developed physical marks when they re-experienced traumas under hypnosis. Reincarnation cases indicate that such effects can even persist into the next life. The traumas can "scar" the consciousness to such an extent that the scars affect the next body that it occupies.

The long-lasting effects of the trauma may seem odd at first, until we remember the way that traumatic events can affect the mind in this life. People who experience significant emotional or physical trauma can develop post-traumatic stress disorder in which they experience physical and emotional symptoms years after the original event occurred. We should not be surprised then to learn that such traumas can travel with the consciousness into the next life, whether as scars or as phobias. We might hope that all our past difficulties would disappear when one life ended, but these cases indicate that they do not.

The When and Where of Reincarnation

Now let us consider whether the surviving consciousness has any control over when and where it is reborn. In a number of cases, the children have reported that they chose their next parents. In the Asian cases, they sometimes describe an episode in which they see one of their future parents and decide to follow that person home to join the family. In the American cases, the children may talk about being in heaven and picking their next parents. Although those stories are obviously unverifiable, some of the Asian ones have been at least partially verified in that the parent had been in the area described by the child around the time of conception.

In other cases, when we think of how bitterly the children complain about the family that they are in, we may conclude that they show no sign of having chosen their parents. Since most of the children do not report any memories of the time between lives, we get no indication from them if they were involved in any decision-making or not. It is possible that they were but do not have access to the memory of being so. We have no way of knowing for sure, but given the variety of cases, it is possible that some individuals choose their parents or their place of rebirth while others do not.

This brings up the larger question of whether anybody at all makes decisions in the process of reincarnation. If the individual consciousness does not decide when to be reborn, do guides, angels, or gods decide? Or does it occur naturally without any conscious decision-making? Various belief systems have different scenarios for how the individual goes on to the next life. Though a few of our subjects talk about guides directing them to their current family, most of them do not say anything about the time between lives, so our cases really shed very little light on this important question.

Along these lines, we can look specifically at the location of rebirths. One conclusion we can draw from these cases is that the place where the rebirth occurs, at least in situations in which the child retains memories of the previous life, is not random. The vast majority of the children report past lives in the same country of their current life, and many of them say that they lived in the same village or even in the same family. What are we to make of this? One possibility is that geographical constraints affect where the consciousness can go to be reborn. Though the idea that consciousness would be limited to a small area seems odd, it fits with the stories by some children of staying in a particular location, the place where the previous personality died for instance, until they saw one of their future parents.

I am more inclined to believe that consciousness is drawn to particular areas because of emotional connections with them. Many of us identify strongly with being from a particular country, so we might naturally be more likely to be reborn in the same country. In addition, people may have emotional attachments to particular places and would be drawn to return to them. Most importantly, an individual's connections to other people may play a big role in where the rebirth occurs. In the same-family cases, the children may be reborn in the family because a strong emotional connection has continued. Particularly in cases in which the previous personality was a child who died young, the individual consciousness may still be closely tied to the family, so it is drawn to be reborn in it. The mechanism of how it is drawn is of course a mystery, but I can imagine an emotional force in the world of consciousness that would draw individuals to particular places or families with an almost magnetic pull.

The cases in which the children report past lives from other countries offer possible insight into this. In these cases, the children usually say that they died in their past life in the country where they currently live, an example being Burmese children who say they were Japanese soldiers killed in Burma during World War II. Many of those Burmese children express a longing to return to Japan, as if they were trapped in Burma after dying there. We do not know if they were trapped there by geographical limitations or by emotional ties. Their actions as soldiers, many of whom were very harsh with the Burmese people, may have created an unresolved emotional connection that caused them to stay in Burma for their next life.

Whether the explanation is geographical or emotional, we can say that these cases show that individuals often keep some links with a life after the end of it. We do not know if this is true in general or just in the cases with preserved memories, but these cases demonstrate that in some situations links do continue into the next life. In the cases of Burmese children who report memories as Japanese soldiers, a link is maintained with both Burma and Japan, as the children are born in Burma but still long for Japan.

The Question of Karma

Karma is a concept that is part of many religions that have a belief in reincarnation, notably Hinduism and Buddhism. It includes many subtleties in the various religious systems that we are not able to discuss here, but in general, it is the belief that an individual's actions determine his or her future circumstances. This includes the idea that actions in previous lives affect an individual's circumstances in the current one. One interpretation of the Burmese-Japanese cases I just mentioned is that their past actions against Burmese people caused them to be reborn as Burmese individuals.

Do our cases in general provide any evidence for the existence of karma? Before answering that question, I should point out that with karma, an individual's circumstances in the current life are thought to be due not just to actions in the last life but also to actions in any of the previous lives, so assessing the effects of those in only the last life is difficult.

I looked at our computer database to see if any characteristics of the previous personality would correlate with the circumstances that the subject was born into. Specifically, I looked at the following items about the previous personality—Was PP saintly? Was PP a criminal? Did PP commit moral transgressions? Was PP philanthropic or generous? And was PP active in religious observances?—to see if any of them correlated with the economic status of the subject, the social status of the subject, or the caste of the subject for Indian cases. In doing so, I am aware that we would consider a child with loving, supportive, but poor parents to be born into positive circumstances, but we might at least think that positive circumstances would be more likely to include higher economic settings than lower ones.

When I ran the correlation tests, only one of the characteristics of the previous personality correlated with the circumstances of the subject. Saintliness in the previous personality showed a very strong correlation with the economic status of the subject and a significant correlation with the social status of the subject. This means that the more saintly the previous personality was considered to have been, the higher the economic status and social status that the child is likely to have. Saintliness did not correlate with the caste of the subject in the cases in India, and none of the other characteristics of the previous personality correlated with the circumstances of the subject. We have to consider then that the correlations that the saintliness item shows may just be a statistical fluke, and we have little evidence that karma from the previous life affects the circumstances of the rebirth.

Another factor that argues against karmic effects is one that I mentioned in Chapter 4. The birthmark and birth defect cases involve lesions that match wounds that the children remember suffering in the previous life. If we thought that karma was responsible for them, then we might expect them to match wounds that the previous personalities inflicted on someone else rather than ones that they suffered themselves. Since this is not the case, we have to say that the marks and defects do not support the idea of karmic effects.

To repeat, the doctrine of karma is a complex one, and though it may be able to explain the findings covered in this book, we have to conclude that our cases offer very little evidence to support it.

Enduring Emotions

To consider further the possible emotional links, we might like to think that the love and positive emotions we give to others can last more than one lifetime, and the cases give us hope that they may. Not only do birthmarks and phobias occur in these cases, but the children also continue to express love for the previous family. Love endures.

This seems particularly evident in the same-family cases. William, the boy in Chapter 1, told his mother that he would always take care of her, just as his grandfather had told her. Patrick Christenson, the boy in Chapter 4 with multiple birthmarks, talked about when he left his mother at the end of the short life of her first son, and he has a very close relationship with her now. Such examples indicate that love can survive death and continue into the next life.

Abby Swanson in Chapter 3 said that she had been her great-grandmother. If she was correct, then she came back in a very different relationship with her mother than in the previous time as her grandmother. To go from being grandmother to daughter is quite a change, yet it mirrors what can often happen in a single lifetime when elderly parents eventually come to depend on the children who previously depended on them. Perhaps the question of who is taking care of whom is not as important as the connection that the individuals share. That connection is one that may continue across lifetimes.

Such an idea is not only comforting but may well be true, based on the evidence from many of our cases. The idea of the emotional connection, but not the roles, enduring across lifetimes can affect the way that parents look at their children, because it suggests that parents need to provide discipline for their children, not in a domineering or harsh way, but as guidance for fellow travelers. Children can be seen as equal partners sharing life's journey instead of inferior beings, even though they are partners that need direction and need to feel a sense of security that their parents are in control.

In Abby's case, perhaps her great-grandmother chose to return to Abby's mother so that they could continue their journey together. The roles are different this time, and Abby's mother will need to teach her many things. In the end, she may learn as much from the relationship with Abby as Abby learns from her.

When the rebirth does not occur in the same family, this enduring connection, or at least the longing that it creates, can be a problem in the new life. Many of the children show great emotional upset, because they feel that they are being kept from their real parents. This generally resolves as the children grow older, but it can be very intense when it is present. As I noted in Chapter 6, many of the Asian parents respect what their children say about their past lives since they usually believe them, but they also make clear to the children that the current life is different from the past one. Unfortunately, they sometimes make this point with great emphasis, and some of them use very harsh methods to get their children to stop talking about the previous life.

Even this might be better in the long run than emphasizing

the link to the past life. Relationships from the past life are in the past, and we do not benefit from focusing on past lives to the detriment of the current life. Some of the children certainly experience great distress in wanting to continue the relationships they recall from previous lives, and this can affect their interactions with their current parents. Similarly, some adults get so caught up in the possibility of their past lives that they neglect to experience the current one. Surely, this is not the best course to take. While being aware of the possibility of reincarnation may make people more appreciative of the spiritual aspects of life and of the spiritual component of others, people should not focus too much on possible past lives.

Along these lines, some people undergo hypnotic past-life regression to try to uncover their past lives. Even if people could gain from exploring their past lives, little evidence exists to support using hypnotic regression to do so. Many hypnotists can place subjects under hypnosis and get them to recall apparent memories from the past, often with great detail and emotion. The hard part comes in trying to verify that these "memories" are of events that actually happened. In many cases, the subject has appeared to remember a life from ancient times, so determining whether it actually occurred is impossible. In others, the subject's report has included historical absurdities. Additionally, in some cases, subjects have recalled details that were then discovered to have come from another source, such as a book they had read years before and forgotten about.

I discussed cases in Chapter 8 in which hypnosis produced some dramatic results, but unfortunately, it is a very unreliable tool, whether being used to uncover memories from the present life or from past ones. Hypnosis can lead to some remarkable memories from the present life, but it can also produce fantasy material. Under hypnosis, the mind tends to fill in the blanks. If a person is being asked to give details that he or she does not remember, the mind will usually come up with some. Once this has happened, the person may then have great difficulty distinguishing actual memories from fantasy ones.

This is not to say that all hypnotic past-life regression cases are worthless. After all, if some young children can have memories of previous lives, then logic would dictate that some adults may be able to discover such memories through the use of hypnosis just as they can pull up early childhood memories. Even so, the vast majority of cases contain no evidence supporting the idea that the images people see under hypnosis are ones from actual past lives that they led. As Alan Gauld has written, though a few strong cases may be found, "they will be so small a solid residue from so great a flood of entertaining but inconclusive eyewash, that one would be ill-advised to waste one's lifetime in attempting to induce them."

Advice for Parents

Parents frequently ask us for advice on how to handle their children's statements about past lives. Though each case has individual differences, I can offer some general guidance that I hope will be helpful. First, parents should know that these statements do not indicate mental illness. We have talked with many families in which a child claimed to remember another set of parents, another home, or a previous death, and the children rarely show any mental health problems.

Several studies have looked at this question. I recently completed a study with a colleague, Dr. Don Nidiffer, in which we looked at psychological testing results of fifteen young American subjects. They were between the ages of three and six years old at the time of the testing, and we found that they were generally quite intelligent. When we looked at scales measuring problem behaviors, their averages were all in the normal range, and they did not show any evidence of psychological problems.

These results are similar to ones that Erlendur Haraldsson and his colleagues have found when they tested subjects in other countries. In Sri Lanka, the subjects also did very well in school but showed some mild behavioral problems at home. Most significantly, they were not more suggestible than other children, arguing against the idea that they claimed memories of a past life because other people had suggested that they had one. In Lebanon, the children also showed no clinically relevant symptoms, though they tended to daydream a lot. The testing again showed that the subjects were not unusually suggestible. Overall, the children appear to be functioning quite well.

When children talk about a past life, parents are sometimes unsure how to respond. We recommend that parents be open to what their children are reporting. Some of the children show emotional intensity regarding these issues, and parents should be respectful in listening just as they are with other topics that their children bring up.

When a child talks about a past life, parents should avoid asking a lot of pointed questions. This could be upsetting to the child and, more importantly from our standpoint, could lead the child to make up answers to the questions. Separating memories from fantasy would then be difficult or impossible. Asking general, open-ended questions such as, "Do you remember anything else?" is fine, and empathizing with a child's statements—"That must have been scary," for instance, when a child describes a fatal accident—certainly is as well.

We encourage parents to write down any statements about a past life that their children make. This is particularly important in cases in which the children give enough information so that identifying a particular deceased individual might be possible. In such a situation, having the statements recorded ahead of time would be critical in providing the best evidence that the child actually recalled events from a previous life.

At the same time, parents should not become so focused on the statements that they and their children lose sight of the fact that the current life is what is most important now. If children persist in saying they want their old family or old home, explaining that their current family is the one they have for this life may be helpful. Parents should acknowledge and value what their children have told them while making clear that the past life is truly in the past.

Parents are sometimes more upset by the statements than their child is. Hearing a child describe the experience of dying in a painful or difficult way can be hard, but both parent and child can know that the child is safe now in this life. Some parents may be comforted to know that the vast majority of these children stop talking about a previous life by the time they are five to seven years old. As I have mentioned, the memories will persist into adolescence or adulthood on rare occasions, but they are usually much less intense then than they were during the younger years. In many cases, as children get older, they do not even remember that they ever talked about a past life.

Overall, parents often find children's claims to remember previous lives more remarkable than do the children, for whom the apparent memories are simply part of their experience of life. The children then move on from the memories to lead typical childhoods.

Spiritual Speculations

Our cases contribute to the evidence that consciousness can survive death in at least some situations, and this is surely a more important finding than any specific ones that we may discern. This means that each of us is more than just a physical body. We have a consciousness as well that is capable of surviving the death of that body. If we change the terminology from consciousness to spirit, then we can say that we all have a spiritual component along with our physical bodies.

If we conclude that every person we meet is a spiritual being as well as a physical one, can we use this knowledge to change the way we treat each other? We might think that we could, but as a monk, Swami Muklyananda, once told Dr. Stevenson, "We in India know that reincarnation occurs, but it makes no difference. Here in India we have just as many rogues and villains as you have in the West." Dr. Stevenson points out that though this is probably correct on the whole, the belief in reincarnation can certainly make a difference for an individual who accepts all that the doctrine involves.

I do hope that having awareness that we each have a spiritual component that may need attention and care just as the physical part of us does could make a difference. An exclusive focus on the physical may keep us from seeing what we need to do to foster our spiritual side, and it may also tend to make us more competitive and selfish in our interactions with others. Surely, we can learn to be less materialistic if we understand that a larger spiritual world is available to us. Fully accepting that we are all spiritual beings will clearly take more than just knowing about reincarnation research, but having that knowledge may enable people to explore ways of living a more spiritual life.

To consider another issue: If those of us who do not remember previous lives do reincarnate, then some emotional issues may come with us even if specific memories do not. Babies are born with different temperaments and different emotional reactions to things. This leads biologists to focus on how our genes may affect our emotions, but we can wonder if a consciousness or spiritual component that brings emotions with it from previous lives is involved as well. If so, this implies that we may have multiple lifetimes to work through difficult emotional issues. Though the idea of carrying emotional baggage from one life to the next may seem unpleasant, the prospect of having more than one lifetime to deal with it also suggests that we may be able eventually to resolve more issues than we know. The concept of reincarnation is compelling to many people because of the idea that an individual can live multiple lives and accumulate wisdom, becoming more loving and peaceful in successive lives. Though we should not expect perfection even after multiple lives, we can surely get closer if we have more than one life in which to make progress.

At the risk of sounding philosophical, we can speculate further that such reasoning also suggests that our purpose in life can change from one lifetime to the next. We may not find one single "meaning of life" but rather different purposes in each life. One individual may be working on very different emotional issues from another person, and thus we see some people content to invest all their energy in connecting with their loved ones. Other people are content to be alone while focusing on asserting themselves in the work world. Perhaps we all take turns working on different aspects of ourselves until we get closer to getting it right. The idea that we get more than one crack at life and that we do not have to get everything sorted through in one lifetime is certainly appealing, but the hard part for some people comes in developing a sense of purpose of any kind in their lives. This is a task for us whether we live one life or more than one, but it may seem less daunting if we decide that developing a sense of purpose in one aspect of life is enough for this time around. We do not have to participate in every type of experience or success in one lifetime in order for it to have value.

Future Research

Even after forty years of research, our work here is still very much unfinished. I am planning to continue to focus primarily on American cases of past-life memories. Along with doing studies in which we look at particular facets of the cases, I hope that as more people hear about our work, we will be able to conduct investigations of more American cases and stronger American cases. If we could study cases in the United States as strong as the best of Asia, then the work would be very hard for people to dismiss. Cases have been harder to find here, but I remain optimistic that at some point, we will have a collection of cases that are so well documented that we can confidently answer the question of whether some children are able to remember previous lives.

We may also have another tool at our disposal in the future to help answer that question. A number of researchers have looked at how the brain functions in recalling actual memories compared to false ones—things that people think they remember happening that actually did not. The work is preliminary at this point. It has involved showing people lists of words. They are then shown a word and asked whether it was on the previous list. Sometimes, the people think they remember seeing the word on the list when they actually did not. Thus, they have a false memory. The researchers have done brain imaging studies in which they measure brain activity when the people are recalling the false memories compared to when they are recalling actual memories, and they have found that different parts of the brain are active during the different recalls. If this research progresses enough so that such testing could determine whether particular individuals have accurate memories of events from earlier in their lives, then we might be able to use it to evaluate memories of previous lives as well. This would be years off, if ever, but it is an intriguing possibility.

If we do eventually establish, to our own satisfaction at least, that some children are able to recall events from previous lives, then we can move on to explore further the questions in this chapter. We would love to learn more about the process of reincarnation, if it occurs, and I hope that this knowledge would then enable people to make positive changes in how they live their lives.

Other work is going on at the Division of Personality Studies at the University of Virginia. Dr. Bruce Greyson, who is now the director of the division, focuses primarily on near-death experiences. One of his current studies involves placing a laptop computer high in a hospital treatment room in which patients have heart defibrillators implanted. Since heart arrhythmias that could normally be fatal are induced in these patients during the procedure, Dr. Greyson is looking to see if any of them will have a near-death experience and be able to describe the particular screensaver displayed on the laptop computer during their procedure.

Dr. Emily Kelly conducts research looking at a variety of unusual experiences, including apparitions and death-bed visions. She is currently doing a study with mediums in which they describe messages that they say deceased individuals want to convey to particular volunteers who have deceased loved ones, and the mediums must give this report without getting any feedback from the volunteers at all. In fact, they never even meet or talk to the volunteers. If they produce accurate information, we will know that they did not infer it from anything that the volunteers did or said.

These studies are exciting, and we hope to continue to make advances in considering the possibility of survival after death. The Division of Personality Studies is still dependent on donations to fund much of its day-to-day operation. When money has been plentiful, the division has been able to perform more research projects, and during lean times, activities and personnel have had to be cut back. The state of Virginia does not contribute to the work at the division, and the generosity of people like Chester Carlson, along with other individuals and private foundations that have made substantial donations, is what has made this research possible. We hope to be fortunate enough to continue and even expand the work that we are doing to look at this most interesting question of life after death.

Final Thoughts

If we are able one day to answer definitively the question of whether we can survive death, I hope that this work with young children will be an important part of that answer. If it is, then that will demonstrate that the smallest and youngest among us have wisdom to share with everyone else—they may be "old souls" in new bodies. If we are all spiritual beings, we should aspire to treat others with all the respect that this implies, and treating children with such respect must include listening to them. Just as the children in this book may have important knowledge to impart to us, so may others if we are ready to listen to these small fellow travelers on this most remarkable road of life.

Out of the mouth of babes . . .

AUTHOR'S NOTE

I would like to hear from parents of children who have reported memories of a previous life, if they are willing to be interviewed about their experiences. Our e-mail address is DOPS@virginia.edu and our postal address is:

Division of Personality Studies
University of Virginia Health System
P.O. Box 800152
Charlottesville, VA 22908-0152.

All cases will be handled confidentially, as we always conceal the identities of families in any reports that we publish.

ACKNOWLEDGMENTS

First and foremost, I want to thank Ian Stevenson, whose work provided the foundation for much of this book. He has been an inspiring pioneer and a wonderful mentor. He gave me the opportunity to participate in this field despite my lack of research experience, and he has continued to provide much support and encouragement for my efforts. His books were also important resources for this one. In particular, I found his overview of the work, *Children Who Remember Previous Lives,* to be very helpful.

Many thanks go to the families who have cooperated with our research. Not only have they demonstrated tolerance for our many questions, but they have even shown great hospitality as we intruded on their time. Similarly, our interpreters in the various countries have been indispensable, and they have always maintained positive attitudes despite long work days on the road. I want to thank the other researchers in this field, whose cases are included both in the overall statistics I cite and, at times, in the individual case write-ups. They are Erlendur Haraldsson, Jürgen Keil, Antonia Mills, and Satwant Pasricha. Thanks as well to Carol Bowman, who referred several of the cases in this book to us, and to the Bial Foundation, which provided a grant that funded several of the American investigations.

I am grateful to my literary agent, Patricia Van der Leun, who found a publisher for me in a remarkably short period of time, and to my editor, Diane Reverand, who helped me make countless improvements in the text. In addition, Martha Stockhausen, my former research assistant, offered many helpful suggestions about several of the chapters. I owe thanks also to Raymond Moody, whose classic work on near-death experiences, *Life After Life,* inspired the title of this book.

Finally, I want to thank my wife, Chris, who acts as my unofficial editor, my colleague, my support, my soul mate. While I would love to spend multiple lifetimes with her, I feel so very fortunate to share even one.

NOTES

Introduction

p. xi: The case of Kemal Atasoy: Keil & Tucker, 2005.

1: Children Who Report Memories of Previous Lives

p. 4: between 20 and 27 percent: see Gallup, with Proctor, 1982; Inglehart, Basañez, and Moreno, 1998; and the Taylor references.

p. 4: a similar percentage of Europeans: Walter & Waterhouse, 1999.

p. 4: a Harris poll in 2003: Taylor, 2003.

p. 7: making a prediction: Stevenson, 2001, pp. 98–99.

p. 8: the current Dalai Lama: Dalai Lama, 1962, pp. 23–24.

p. 8: Of forty-six cases: Stevenson, 1966.

p. 8: Victor Vincent: Stevenson, 1974, pp. 259–69.

p. 9: Süleyman Çaper: Stevenson, 1997a, pp. 1429–42.

p. 11: Suzanne Ghanem: Dr. Stevenson, who investigated Suzanne Ghanem's case, has not published a case report on it, but she is featured in Chapters 6 and 8 of Shroder, 1999.

p. 14: Parmod Sharma: Stevenson, 1974, pp. 109–27.

p. 15: Shamlinie Prema: Stevenson, 1977a, pp. 15–42.

2: Investigating the Cases

p. 17: Dr. Ian Stevenson: For more information on Dr. Stevenson's career, see Stevenson, 1989 and Shroder, 1999.

p. 17: "The Evidence for Survival": Stevenson, 1960.

p. 18: "These forty-four cases": Shroder, 1999, p. 103.

p. 20: "in regard to reincarnation": King, 1975, p. 978.

p. 20: "He has placed on record": ibid.

p. 20: "a methodical, careful": Lief, 1977, p. 171.

p. 20: "Either he is making": ibid.

p. 27: Dr. Keil eventually: Keil & Tucker, 2000.

3: Explanations to Consider

p. 33: The following list: For another discussion of the possible explanations, see Chapter 7 in Stevenson, 2001.

p. 39: The argument goes: This so-called socio-psychological hypothesis is described in Stevenson & Samararatne, 1988. For another discussion of it, see Brody, 1979.

p. 39: Bishen Chand Kapoor: Stevenson, 1975, pp. 176–205.

p. 44: research that has been done in parapsychology: A number of good reviews are available, including Radin, 1997.

4: Marked for Life

p. 55: The case of Chanai Choomalaiwong: Stevenson, 1997a, pp. 300–23.

p. 57: The case of Necip Ünlütaşkiran: Stevenson, 1997a, pp. 430–55.

p. 59: a shotgun blast: Hanumant Saxena in Stevenson, 1997a, pp. 455–67.

p. 60: The case of Indika Ishwara: Stevenson, 1997a, pp. 1970–2000.

p. 64: The case of Purnima Ekanayake: Haraldsson, 2000.

p. 67: stress can contribute: See Sternberg, 2000, for a detailed overview of this area.

p. 68: one notable case: Moody, 1946.

p. 74: a boy in Sri Lanka named Wijeratne: Stevenson, 1997a, pp. 1366–73.

p. 77: the Dalai Lama wrote: The Dalai Lama, 1962.

p. 77: Dr. Stevenson describes twenty: Stevenson, 1997a, pp. 803–79.

p. 77: Jürgen Keil and I found: Tucker & Keil, in press.

p. 78: Kloy Matwiset: Tucker & Keil, 2001.

5: Remembering the Past

p. 86: Sujith Jayaratne: Stevenson, 1977a, pp. 235–80.
p. 90: Dr. James Matlock: Matlock, 1989.
p. 96: The case of Kumkum Verma: Stevenson, 1975, pp. 206–40.
p. 98: The case of Jagdish Chandra: Stevenson, 1975, pp. 144–75.
p. 101: The case of Ratana Wongsombat: Stevenson, 1983, pp. 12–48.
p. 102: The case of Gamini Jayasena: Stevenson, 1977a, pp. 43–76.

6: Unusual Behaviors

p. 116: Sukla Gupta: Stevenson, 1974. pp. 52–67.
p. 117: Maung Aye Kyaw: Stevenson, 1997a, pp. 212–26.
p. 118: Bongkuch Promsin: Stevenson, 1983, pp. 109–39.
p. 118: Fear-death Experiences: Dr. Stevenson and colleagues (Stevenson, Cook, & McClean-Rice, 1989–90) coined this term to refer to near-death experiences that occur when people fear they are going to die but do not actually approach physiological death. I am using it differently here to highlight the fears that our subjects show about the mode of the previous death.
p. 118: a phobia that relates: for more details, see Stevenson, 1990.
p. 119: Shamlinie Prema: Stevenson, 1977a, pp. 15–42.
p. 120: Jasbir Singh: Stevenson, 1974, pp. 34–52.
p. 121: Ma Tin Aung Myo: Stevenson, 1983, pp. 229–41.
p. 121: Carl Edon: Stevenson, 2003, pp. 67–74. Dr. Nicholas McLean-Rice investigated the case along with Dr. Stevenson.
p. 122: Swaran Lata: Pasricha & Stevenson, 1977.
p. 122: children's play: For more on subjects' play, see Stevenson, 2000.
p. 123: Maung Myint Soe: Stevenson, 1997a, pp. 1403–10.
p. 123: Ramez Shams: Stevenson, 1997a, p. 1406.
p. 124: one series of sex-change cases: Stevenson, 1997a.
p. 125: current thinking about gender identity disorder: References are included in the case report on Kloy Matwiset: Tucker & Keil, 2001.
p. 126: Erin Jackson: Stevenson, 2001, pp. 87–89.
p. 129: The case of the Pollock twins: Stevenson, 1997a, pp. 2041–58 and Stevenson, 2003, pp. 89–93.
p. 132: temperament: Thomas & Chess, 1984.

p. 134: suffering in other cases: Stevenson, 2001, p. 217.

p. 134: Bishen Chand Kapoor: Stevenson, 1974, pp. 176–205 and Stevenson, 2001, p. 303.

p. 134: Marta Lorenz: Stevenson, 1974, 183–203.

p. 134: "Emilia is not in the cemetery": Stevenson, 1974: pp. 187, 196.

p. 134: "Don't say that": Stevenson, 1974: p. 187.

p. 134: relief that can occur: Stevenson, 2001, p. 281.

7: Recognizing Familiar Faces

p. 144: As Dr. Stevenson has written: Stevenson, 2001.

p. 147: The case of Nazih Al-Danaf: Haraldsson & Abu-Izzeddin, 2002.

p. 151: The case of Gnanatilleka Baddewithana: Stevenson, 1974, pp. 131–49 and Nissanka, 2001.

p. 156: The case of Ma Choe Hnin Htet: Stevenson, 1997a, pp. 839–52.

8: Divine Intermission

p. 169: a scale that rates: Tucker, 2000.

p. 169: Poonam Sharma: Sharma & Tucker, 2005.

p. 170: Veer Singh: Stevenson, 1975, pp. 312–36.

p. 171: Bongkuch Promsin: Stevenson, 1983, pp. 102–39.

p. 172: Disna Samarasinghe: Stevenson, 1977a, pp. 77–116.

p. 173: Sunita Khandelwal: Stevenson, 1997a, pp. 468–91.

p. 178: "Most scientists probably": Rovee-Collier, 1997, p. 468.

p. 179: last longer and are more specific: Rovee-Collier & Hayne, 2000.

p. 179: "The growing consensus": Howe, 2000, p. 19.

p. 179: the inability to retain: Rovee-Collier, Hartshorn & DiRubbo, 1999.

p. 180: a child was able: Myers, Clifton & Clarkson, 1987.

p. 180: researchers interviewed ten children: Fivush, Gray & Fromhoff, 1987.

p. 180: researchers asked pregnant women: DeCasper & Spence, 1986.

p. 181: In one report: Cheek, 1992.

p. 182: Dr. Cheek thought that: Cheek, 1996.

9: Opposing Points of View

p. 185: "The trouble with people": People have attributed various versions of this line to a number of individuals, notably Will Rogers, as Walter Mondale did in a 1984 debate with Ronald Reagan. *Respectfully Quoted* from the Library of Congress (Platt, 1989) credits Josh Billings as the most likely author.
p. 185: various religious beliefs: Almeder makes this distinction in Almeder, 1997.
p. 186: "At the time of writing": Sagan, 1996, p. 302.
p. 188: "this confrontation between": Dennett, 1991, p. 35.
p. 188: "This argument depends": Stapp, 2005, p. 45.
p. 188: "yet it is fully": Stapp, 1993, p. 23.
p. 188: quantum mechanics: For an overview of quantum mechanics, see Greene, 1999.
p. 188: He and quantum physicist Friedrich Beck: Eccles, 1994, Chapter 9.
p. 188: Elizabeth Rauscher and Russell Targ: Rauscher & Targ, 2001, and Rauscher & Targ, 2002.
p. 189: clearly implied by theoretical physics: Costa de Beauregard, 1987, p. 569.
p. 189: precognition, telepathy, and psychokinesis: Costa de Beauregard, 1998.
p. 189: "far from being": Costa de Beauregard, 2002, p. 653.
p. 189: "these developments may": Klarreich, 2001, p. 339.
p. 189: in the long run: Josephson & Pallikari-Viras, 1991, p. 199.
p. 189: the importance of consciousness: The material in these two paragraphs is from Folger, 2002.
p. 190: "I cannot imagine": ibid, p. 48.
p. 191: "it is difficult": Radin & Nelson, 1989, p. 1512.
p. 192: At last count: Benor, 2001.
p. 192: heart disease: Byrd, 1988 and Harris, et al., 1999.
p. 192: AIDS: Sicher, et al., 1998.
p. 192: One review found: Astin, Harkness, & Ernst, 2000.
p. 193: Does other evidence: For a brief review, see Stevenson, 1977b.
p. 193: near-death experiences: See Greyson & Flynn, 1984 and Moody, 1975/2001 for more on near-death experiences.
p. 193: Pam Reynolds: Sabom, 1998. Also, Broome, 2003.
p. 193: Al Sullivan: Cook, et al., 1998.
p. 193: reports of apparitions: Stevenson, 1982.

p. 194: Research with mediums: The information on Mrs. Piper and Mrs. Leonard comes from Gauld, 1982.
p. 195: recent studies: Schwartz (with Simon), 2002.
p. 195: "consilience": Wilson, 1998, p. 8.
p. 195: "the explanations": Wilson, 1998, p. 53.
p. 195: how could stones: The quote "Stones cannot fall from the sky, because there are no stones in the sky" is often attributed to the great chemist Antoine Lavoisier, but I could not find solid documentation that he actually said it.
p. 195: Ignaz Semmelweis: Lyons & Petrucelli, 1987 and Bender, 1966.
p. 196: "If we are": Plate tectonics, 2002.
p. 199: David Bishai: Bishai, 2000.
p. 199: 105 billion human beings: The calculation is in Haub, 1995.
p. 200: William James looked: James, 1898/1956.
p. 202: Second Council of Constantinople: Head & Cranston, 1977, pp. 156–60.

10: Conclusions and Speculations

p. 206: In the first one: Stevenson & Keil, 2000.
p. 207: Dr. Sybo Schouten: Schouten & Stevenson, 1998.
p. 211: "reincarnation is the best": Stevenson, 2001, p. 254.
p. 211: we know almost nothing: ibid.
p. 216: "psychophore": Stevenson, 2001, p. 234.
p. 216: Their doctrine of *anatta*: This description summarizes Dr. Stevenson's discussion of *anatta* in Stevenson, 1977a, pp. 3–5.
p. 217: most practicing Buddhists: Head & Cranston, 1977, pp. 63–66.
p. 225: the subject has appeared: Gauld, 1982, pp. 166–71.
p. 226: "they will be": Gauld, 1982, p. 171.
p. 227: In Sri Lanka: Haraldsson, 1995; Haraldsson, 1997; Haraldsson, Fowler & Periyannanpillai, 2000.
p. 227: In Lebanon: Haraldsson, 2003.
p. 229: "We in India": Stevenson, 2001, p. 232.
p. 234: "Out of the mouth of babes": *The Holy Bible: King James Version,* Psalms 8:2.

REFERENCES

Almeder, R. 1997. A critique of arguments offered against reincarnation. *Journal of Scientific Exploration* 11(4): 499–526.

Astin, J. A., E. Harkness, and E. Ernst, 2000. The efficacy of "distant healing": A systematic review of randomized trials. *Annals of Internal Medicine* 132(11):903–10.

Bender, G. A. 1966. *Great moments in medicine.* Detroit: Northwood Institute Press.

Benor, D. J. 2001. *Spiritual healing: Scientific validation of a healing revolution.* Southfield, Mich.: Vision Publications.

Bishai, D. 2000. Can population growth rule out reincarnation? A model of circular migration. *Journal of Scientific Exploration* 14(3):411–20.

Bowman, C. 1997. *Children's past lives: How past life memories affect your child.* New York: Bantam Books.

Bowman, C. 2001. *Return from heaven: Beloved relatives reincarnated within your family.* New York: HarperCollins.

Brody, E. B. 1979. Review of *Cases of the reincarnation type. Vol. II: Ten cases in Sri Lanka* by Ian Stevenson. *Journal of Nervous and Mental Disease* 167:769–74.

Broome, K. (producer). 2003, February 5. *The day I died* [Television broadcast]. London: BBC Two.

Byrd, R. 1988. Positive therapeutic effects of intercessory prayer in a coronary care unit population. *Southern Medical Journal* 81(7):826–29.

Cheek, D. B. 1992. Are telepathy, clairvoyance and "hearing" possible in utero? Suggestive evidence as revealed during hypnotic age-regression studies of prenatal memory. *Pre- and Perinatal Psychology Journal* 7(2):125–37.

Cheek, D. B. 1996. An interview with David Cheek, M.D. Interview by Michael D. Yapko. *American Journal of Clinical Hypnosis* 39(1):2–17.

Cook, E. W., B. Greyson, and I. Stevenson. 1998. Do any near-death experiences provide evidence for the survival of human personality after death? Relevant features and illustrative case reports. *Journal of Scientific Exploration* 12(3):377–406.

Costa de Beauregard, O. 1987. According to "physical irreversibility," the "paranormal" is not de jure suppressed, but is de facto repressed. *Behavioral and Brain Sciences* 10(4):569–70.

Costa de Beauregard, O. 1998. The paranormal is not excluded from physics. *Journal of Scientific Exploration* 12(2):315–20.

Costa de Beauregard, O. 2002. Wavelike coherence and CPT invariance: Sesames of the Paranormal. *Journal of Scientific Exploration* 16(4):651–54.

Dalai Lama. 1962. *My land and my people: Autobiography of the Dalai Lama.* New York: McGraw-Hill.

DeCasper, A. J. and M. J. Spence. 1986. Prenatal maternal speech influences newborns' perception of speech sounds. *Infant Behavior & Development* 9(2): 133–50.

Dennett, D. C. 1991. *Consciousness explained.* Boston: Little, Brown.

Eccles, J. C. 1994. *How the self controls its brain.* Berlin: Springer-Verlag.

Fivush, R., J. T. Gray, and F. A. Fromhoff. 1987. Two-year-olds talk about the past. *Cognitive Development* 2:393–409.

Folger, T. 2002. Does the universe exist if we're not looking? *Discover* June:44–48.

Gallup, G., with W. Proctor. 1982. *Adventures in immortality*. New York: McGraw-Hill.

Gauld, A. 1982. *Mediumship and survival: A century of investigations*. London: William Heinemann.

Greene, B. 1999. *The elegant universe: Superstrings, hidden dimensions, and the quest for the ultimate theory*. New York: W. W. Norton.

Greyson, B. and C. P. Flynn, eds. 1984. *The near-death experience: Problems, prospects, perspectives*. Springfield, Ill.: Charles C. Thomas.

Haraldsson, E. 1995. Personality and abilities of children claiming previous-life memories. *Journal of Nervous and Mental Disease* 183(7):445–51.

Haraldsson, E. 1997. A psychological comparison between ordinary children and those who claim previous-life memories. *Journal of Scientific Exploration* 11(3):323–35.

Haraldsson, E. 2000. Birthmarks and claims of previous-life memories: I. The case of Purnima Ekanayake. *Journal of the Society for Psychical Research* 64(858):16–25.

Haraldsson, E. 2003. Children who speak of past-life experiences: Is there a psychological explanation? *Psychology and Psychotherapy: Theory, Research and Practice* 76:55–67.

Haraldsson, E. and M. Abu-Izzeddin. 2002. Development of certainty about the correct deceased person in a case of the reincarnation type in Lebanon: The case of Nazih Al-Danaf. *Journal of Scientific Exploration* 16:363–80.

Haraldsson, E., P. C. Fowler, and V. Periyannanpillai. 2000. Psychological characteristics of children who speak of a previous life: A further field study in Sri Lanka. *Transcultural Psychiatry* 37(4):525–44.

Harris, W. S., M. Gowda, J. W. Kolb, C. P. Strychacz, J. L. Vacek, P. G. Jones, A. Forker, J. H. O'Keefe, and B. D. McCallister. 1999. A randomized, controlled trial of the effects of remote, intercessory prayer on outcomes in patients admitted to the coronary care unit. *Archives of Internal Medicine* 159(19):2273–78.

Haub, C. 1995. How many people have ever lived on earth? *Population Today* 23(2):4–5.

Head, J. and S. L. Cranston. 1977. *Reincarnation: The phoenix fire mystery*. New York: Julian Press/Crown Publishers.

Howe, M. L. 2000. *The fate of early memories: Developmental science and the retention of childhood experiences*. Washington, D.C.: American Psychological Association.

Inglehart, R., M. Basañez, and A. Moreno. 1998. *Human values and beliefs: A cross-cultural sourcebook*. Ann Arbor, Mich.: University of Michigan Press.

James, W. 1898/1956. *Human immortality: Two supposed objections to the doctrine.* 2nd ed. Originally published 1898 Boston: Houghton, Mifflin. Republished in 1956 as *The will to believe and other essays in popular philosophy and human immortality: Two supposed objections to the doctrine*. New York: Dover Publications.

Josephson, B. D. and F. Pallikari-Viras. 1991. Biological utilization of quantum nonlocality. *Foundations of Physics* 21(2):197–207.

Keil, H. H. J. and J. B. Tucker. 2000. An unusual birthmark case thought to be linked to a person who had previously died. *Psychological Reports* 87:1067–74.

Keil, H. H. J. and J. B. Tucker. 2005. Children who claim to remember previous lives: Cases with written records made before the previous personality was identified. *Journal of Scientific Exploration* 19:91–101.

King, L. S. 1975. Reincarnation. *JAMA* 234:978.

Klarreich, E. 2001. Stamp booklet has physicists licked. *Nature* 413:339.

Lief, H. I. 1977. Commentary on Dr. Ian Stevenson's "The evidence of man's survival after death." *Journal of Nervous and Mental Disease* 165:171–73.

Lyons, A. S. and R. J. Petrucelli. 1987. *Medicine: An illustrated history*. New York: Harry N. Abrams.

Matlock, J. G. 1989. Age and stimulus in past life memory cases: A study of published cases. *Journal of the American Society for Psychical Research* 83:303–16.

Moody, R. A. 1975/2001. *Life after life: The investigation of a phenomenon—survival of bodily death*. 2nd ed. New York: HarperSanFrancisco.

Moody, R. L. 1946. Bodily changes during abreaction. *Lancet* 2:934–35.

Myers, N. A., R. K. Clifton, and M. G. Clarkson. 1987. When they were very young: Almost-threes remember two years ago. *Infant Behavior and Development* 10:123–32.

Nissanka, H. S. S. 2001. *The girl who was reborn: A case-study suggestive of reincarnation*. Colombo, Sri Lanka: S. Godage Brothers.

Pasricha, S. and I. Stevenson. 1977. Three cases of the reincarnation type in India. *Indian Journal of Psychiatry* 19:36–42.

Plate tectonics. 2002. In *The new encyclopæadia Britannica* (Vol. 25, p. 886). Chicago: Encyclopæadia Britannica.

Platt, S. ed. 1989. *Respectfully quoted: A dictionary of quotations requested from the congressional research service*. Washington, D.C.: Library of Congress.

Radin, D. 1997. *The conscious universe: The scientific truth of psychic phenomena*. New York: HarperCollins.

Radin, D. I. and R. D. Nelson. 1989. Evidence for consciousness-related anomalies in random physical systems. *Foundations of Physics* 19(12):1499–1514.

Rauscher, E. A. and R. Targ. 2001. The speed of thought: Investigation of a complex space-time metric to describe psychic phenomena. *Journal of Scientific Exploration* 15(3):331–54.

Rauscher, E. A. and R. Targ. 2002. Why only four dimensions will not explain the relationship of the perceived and perceiver in precognition. *Journal of Scientific Exploration* 16(4):655–58.

Rovee-Collier, C. 1997. Dissociations in infant memory: Rethinking the development of implicit and explicit memory. *Psychological Review* 104:467–98.

Rovee-Collier, C., K. Hartshorn, and M. DiRubbo. 1999. Long-term maintenance of infant memory. *Developmental Psychobiology* 35:91–102.

Rovee-Collier, C. and H. Hayne. 2000. Memory in infancy and early childhood. In *The Oxford handbook of memory,* ed. E. Tulving and F. I. M. Craik, 267–82. New York: Oxford University Press.

Sabom, M. 1998. *Light and death: One doctor's fascinating account of near-death experiences*. Grand Rapids, Mich.: Zondervan Publishing House.

Sagan, C. 1996. *The demon-haunted world: Science as a candle in the dark*. New York: Random House.

Schouten, S. A. and I. Stevenson. 1998. Does the socio-psychological hypothesis explain cases of the reincarnation type? *Journal of Nervous and Mental Disease* 186(8):504–6.

Schwartz, G. E., with W. L. Simon. 2002. *The afterlife experiments: Breakthrough scientific evidence of life after death*. New York: Pocket Books.

Sharma, P. and J. B. Tucker. 2005. Cases of the reincarnation type with memories from the intermission between lives. *Journal of Near-Death Studies* 23(2):101–18.

Shroder, T. 1999. *Old souls: The scientific evidence for past lives*. New York: Simon & Schuster.

Sicher, F., E. Targ, D. Moore, and H. S. Smith. 1998. A randomized double-blind study of the effect of distant healing in a population with advanced AIDS. Report of a small scale study. *Western Journal of Medicine* 169(6):356–63.

Stapp, H. P. 1993. *Mind, matter, and quantum mechanics*. Berlin: Springer-Verlag.

Stapp, H. P. 2005. *The mindful universe*. http://www-physics.lbl.gov/~stapp/MUA.pdf (accessed March 14, 2005).

Sternberg, E. M. 2000. *The balance within: The science connecting health and emotions*. New York: W. H. Freeman.

Stevenson, I. 1960. The evidence for survival from claimed memories of former incarnations. *Journal of the American Society for Psychical Research* 54:51–71 and 95–117.

Stevenson, I. 1966. Cultural patterns in cases suggestive of reincarnation among the Tlingit Indians of Southeastern Alaska. *Journal of the American Society for Psychical Research* 60:229–43.

Stevenson, I. 1974. *Twenty cases suggestive of reincarnation*. (rev. ed.) Charlottesville: University Press of Virginia.

Stevenson, I. 1975. *Cases of the reincarnation type, Vol. I: Ten cases in India*. Charlottesville: University Press of Virginia.

Stevenson, I. 1977a. *Cases of the reincarnation type, Vol. II: Ten cases in Sri Lanka*. Charlottesville: University Press of Virginia.

Stevenson, I. 1977b. Research into the evidence of man's survival after death. *Journal of Nervous and Mental Disease* 165(3):152–70.

Stevenson, I. 1980. *Cases of the reincarnation type, Vol. III: Twelve cases in Lebanon and Turkey*. Charlottesville: University Press of Virginia.

Stevenson, I. 1982. The contribution of apparitions to the evidence for survival. *Journal of the American Society for Psychical Research* 76:341–58.

Stevenson, I. 1983. *Cases of the reincarnation type, Vol. IV: Twelve cases in Thailand and Burma*. Charlottesville: University Press of Virginia.

Stevenson, I. 1989. Some of my journeys in medicine. *The Flora Levy lecture in the humanities 1989*. Lafayette, La.: University of Southwestern Louisiana. Also available online at http://www.healthsystem.virginia.edu/personalitystudies/Some-of-My-Journeys-in-Medicine.pdf.

Stevenson, I. 1990. Phobias in children who claim to remember previous lives. *Journal of Scientific Exploration* 4:243–54.

Stevenson, I. 1997a. *Reincarnation and biology: A contribution to the etiology of birthmarks and birth defects*. Westport, Conn.: Praeger.

Stevenson, I. 1997b. *Where reincarnation and biology intersect*. Westport, Conn.: Praeger.

Stevenson, I. 2000. Unusual play in young children who claim to remember previous lives. *Journal of Scientific Exploration* 14:557–70.

Stevenson, I. 2001. *Children who remember previous lives: A question of reincarnation*. (rev. ed.) Jefferson, N.C.: McFarland.

Stevenson, I. 2003. *European cases of the reincarnation type*. Jefferson, N.C.: McFarland.

Stevenson, I., E. W. Cook, and N. McClean-Rice. 1989–90. Are persons reporting "near-death experiences" really near death? A study of medical records. *Omega* 20(1):45–54.

Stevenson, I. and J. Keil. 2000. The stability of assessments of paranormal connections in reincarnation-type cases. *Journal of Scientific Exploration* 14(3):365–82.

Stevenson, I. and G. Samararatne. 1988. Three new cases of the reincarnation type in Sri Lanka with written records made before verification. *Journal of Scientific Exploration* 2:217–38.

Taylor, H. 1998. Large majority of people believe they will go to heaven; only one in fifty thinks they will go to hell. http://www.harrisinteractive.com/harris_poll/index.asp?PID=167 (accessed February 1, 2005).

Taylor, H. 2000. No significant changes in the large majorities who believe in God, heaven, the resurrection, survival of soul, miracles and virgin birth.

http://www.harrisinteractive.com/harris_poll/index.asp?PID=112 (accessed February 1, 2005).

Taylor, H. 2003. The religious and other beliefs of Americans 2003. http://www.harrisinteractive.com/harris_poll/index.asp?PID=359 (accessed February 1, 2005).

Thomas, A. and S. Chess. 1984. Genesis and evolution of behavioral disorders: from infancy to early adult life. *American Journal of Psychiatry* 141:1–9.

Tucker, J. B. 2000. A scale to measure the strength of children's claims of previous lives: Methodology and initial findings. *Journal of Scientific Exploration* 14(4):571–81.

Tucker, J. B. and H. H. J. Keil. 2001. Can cultural beliefs cause a gender identity disorder? *Journal of Psychology & Human Sexuality* 13(2):21–30.

Tucker, J. B. and H. H. J. Keil. in press. Experimental birthmarks: New cases of an Asian practice. *International Journal of Parapsychology.*

Walter, T. and H. Waterhouse. 1999. A very private belief: Reincarnation in contemporary England. *Sociology of Religion* 60(2):187–97.

Wilson, E. O. 1998. *Consilience: The unity of knowledge.* New York: Alfred A. Knopf.